AF540855

UNIVERSITIES AND NGOs

By

Dr. P. Adinarayana Reddy

&

Dr. M.C. Reddeppa Reddy

Department of Adult & Continuing Education

Sri Venkateswara University

Tirupati

DISCOVERY PUBLISHING HOUSE

NEW DELHI-110002

First Published-2006

ISBN 81-8356-130-6

Published by

DISCOVERY PUBLISHING HOUSE
4831/24, Ansari Road, Prahlad Street,
Darya Ganj, New Delhi-110002 (India)
Phone: 23279245 • Fax: 91-11-23253475
E-mail:dphtemp@indiatimes.com

Printed at:

Amit Enterprises

Prof. S. Jayarama Reddy
Vice Chancellor, S.V.U.

Foreword

The extension and delivery services were rendered by the voluntary or non-governmental organisations for a long time in India. But, of late, Universities have taken up the extension activities as its third dimension, the other two being teaching and research. It is through the teaching that the Universities disseminate the knowledge and it is through research that they generate knowledge. The knowledge generated through research is being applied to real life situations and services to the society through the extension services. As the intadels of knowledge covering all areas of knowledge like social, biological, the earth, health and environmental sciences, the Universities can provide practical solutions to many challenges. The society faces time and again. The Universities, with its strong base of knowledge and human resources, can provide technical and human resource support to NGOs. And in turn the NGOs, by means of their advantages of reaching grassroots working with the rural people and implementing action-oriented programmes, will provide apprenticeship training and placements to the University students belonging to various disciplines.

The Universities produce manpower and provide employment whereas the government and non-governmental organisations are the consumers of the University products. As the institutions that provide employment universities have to develop the specialised skills and competencies of the students so as to attain their goals. Hence the Universities and the industries or the NGOs should collaborate together to help the students to learn work-related skills and to procure suitable jobs. Consequentially the rural communities get benefited through the trained and well qualified students.

I am happy to state that our University has initiated steps to interact with the local elite, farming community and industry. A National Conference on University, Industry, Community Interaction was organised on 22nd of December 2005 by the University where the Hon'ble Chief Minister Dr. Y.S. Rajasekhara Reddy inaugurated the Conference. Realising the need for collaboration of University with NGOs; the Department of Adult and Continuing Education organised a Seminar-cum Workshop (5th-6th December 2005) and brought out a book recording the seminar-cum-workshop proceedings.

I congratulate the editors for bringing out a volume of these proceedings and will be useful not only to the University/ Students, but also the NGO functionaries, government personnel and general public.

(S. Jayarama Reddy)
Sri Venkateswara University
Tirupati–517 502
(Andhra Pradesh)

Preface

Recognising the merits of Non Governmental Organisations in terms of involvement, administration, peoples participation and task performance, the Government has chosen them as its partners in implementation of the various development and welfare programmes. As a result of the shift, all the Ministries and Departments have created space for the NGOs in their activities leading to the change in the administration of the programmes. The Universities created for developing the human resources through teaching and research, of late have adopted the extension as their third dimension and are outreaching its resources to the community. Further, the products of the Universities have been utilised by the public, private enterprises and the NGOs to meet their manpower. Hence, all these are performing their tasks in isolation leading to the duplication of the efforts and wastage of resources. Recognising the need for co-ordinated work among universities and NGOs for effective community development and to share the resources, the representatives of the Universities and NGOs were brought to a single platform to pool their experiences and expertise to formulate strategies for manpower development as well as for community development.

The papers are arranged in five sections. Section I, the Linkages between University and NGOs comprises of 11 papers has discussed in detail about the problems, prospects, interventions, present status, future strategies etc., for promoting effective collaboration between universities and NGOs. The role of universities in promotion of Human Resource was discussed by the four authors which are presented in Section II. The Section III contain two papers on Review and

Updating of the curriculum of PG and Diploma courses. Section IV contains 7 papers which dealt on role of NGOs and Universities in Integrated Development. Dissemination of Development and Welfare Programmes in the Community and the role of Universities and NGOs are presented in the last section of the book (4 papers). The outcome of this seminar on Linkages between Universities and NGOs has taken the shape of the book. The Editors of the book express their gratitude to all those who have contributed for seminar and to the present volume. Further, they are grateful to Sri Venkateswara University authorities and to the Universities Grants Commission, New Delhi for providing necessary permission and finance respectively.

P. Adinarayana Reddy

M.C. Reddeppa Reddy

Contents

List of Contributors

Dr. P. Adinarayana Reddy, Director and Head I/c, Department of Adult and Continuing Education, Sri Venkateswara University, Tirupati-517 502.

Dr. Bhalba Vibhute, Director, Department of Adult and Continuing Education, Shivaji University, Kolhapur-416 004.

Dr. K.G. Bharathi, Project Assistant, Department of Adult and Continuing Education, Sri Venkateswara University, Tirupati-517 502.

Dr. J.K. Dixit, Senior Project Officer, Department of Adult and Continuing Education, University of Delhi, Delhi.

Sri. G. Eswaraiah, Research Scholar, Department of Adult and Continuing Education, Sri Venkateswara University, Tirupati-517 502

Dr. A. Janitha Begum, Associate Professor, Department of Education, Periyar University, Salem, Tamil Nadu.

Dr. N. Jayakumar Rao, AMG International, Seethammadhara, Visakhapatnam-13.

Sri. G. Hussain Reddy, Research Scholar, Department of Adult and Continuing Education, Sri Venkateswara University, Tirupati-517 502.

Dr. Kapali, Director, Department of Adult and Continuing Education, Madras University, Chepauk, Chennai.

Dr. T. Kumaraswamy, Assistant Director, Department of Adult and Continuing Education, Sri Venkateswara University, Tirupati-517 502.

Dr. G. Lokanadha Reddy, Professor, Department of Education, Periyar University, Salem, Tamil Nadu.

Dr. V. Narayana Reddy, Associate Professor, Department of Anthroplogy, S.V. University, Tirupati.

Dr. K. Nachimuthu, Associate Professor, Department of Education, Periyar University, Salem, Tamil Nadu.

Dr. A. Paparao, Professor, Department of Anthropology, Sri Venkateswara University, Tirupati-517 502.

Sri K. Penchalaiah, Research Scholar, Department of Anthropology, Sri Venkateswara University, Tirupati-517 502.

Dr. G.V.R.R Prasad, Deputy Director (Retd.), Adult Education, Hyderabad district Hyderabad.

Sri K. Prabhakar, Research Scholar, Department of Anthropology, Sri Venkateswara University, Tirupati-517 502.

Dr. T.G. Ramaiah, National Institute for Rural Development, Rajendra Nagar, Hyderabad.

Sri D. Ramakrishna, Director, RISE, NGO's Colony, Tirupati-517 502.

Sri M. Ramaswami, Akshyashetram, Durgasamudram, Tirupati Rural Mandal.

Dr. M.C. Reddeppa Reddy, Director, Department of Adult and Continuing Education, Sri Venkateswara University, Tirupati-517 502.

Dr. Rajesh, Senior Project Officer, Department of Adult and Continuing Education, University of Delhi, Delhi.

Sri C. Ramakanta Sarma, National Council Member, Public Relations Society of India, 18-1-807, A, Bhavani Nagar, Tirupati.

Dr. V. Reghu, Assistant Director, Department of Adult and Continuing Education, Kerala University, Trivandrum.

Dr. Renuka Narang, Former Director (Rtd.), Department of Adult and Continuing Education, University of Mumbai and Member, UGC Expert, Committee for Adult and Continuing Education, 81-B, Meher Apartment, Ansten Road, Off. Altamount Road, Mumbai-400 026.

Sri M. Subba Rao, Director, MASSES, 25-2-11/32, Revenue Colony, Nellore-500 004.

Dr. K. Sudha Rani, Associate Professor, Department of Adult and Continuing Education, Sri Venkateswara University, Tirupati-517 502.

Dr. S. Sumathi, Assistant Professor, Department of Anthropology, Madras University, Chepauk, Chennai.

Sri. Syam Atluri, Assistant Director, Department of Adult and Continuing Education, Andhra University, Visakahaptnam.

Sri G. Thirupal, Research Scholar, Department of Anthropology, Sri Venkateswara University, Tirupati-517 502.

Dr. D. Uma Devi, Post Doctoral Fellow, Department of Adult and Continuing Education, Sri Venkateswara University, Tirupati-517 502.

Dr. B.S. Vasudeva Rao, Associate Professor, Department of Adult and Continuing Education, Andhra University, Visakhapatnam-530 003.

Dr. N. Venkataiah, Former Head and Dean, Department of Education, Mysore University, Mysore.

Dr. R. Venkata Ravi, Junior Fellow, Council for Social Development 230, Shivanagar Colony, Hyderguda (Post), Rajendra Nagar, Hyderabad-500 048.

S. Vijaya Kumar, Fellow, Council for Social Development, 230, Shivanagar Colony, Hyderguda (Post), Rajendra Nagar, Hyderabad-500 048.

Mrs. G. Vijaya Kumari, P.G. Asst, Govt Hr. Sec. School, R.Pudupalyam, Namakkal, Tamil Nadu.

Mr. P. Viswanadha Gupta Research Scholar, Department of Adult and Continuing Education, Andhra University, Visakhapatnam-530 003.

Theme I

Linkage between Universities and NGOs: Present Status and Future Directions

1

Linkage between Universities and NGOs

K. Nachimuthu
G. Vijaya Kumari

University as the highest level educational institution concerned with generation and dissemination in contemporary society has to be socially relevant and useful for which it is necessary that it must direct all its pursuits in such a manner that its end product may promote the multi-faceted but integrated development of society in which it exists to enable its members to live a healthy and happy life. In the preparation of relevant teaching-learning material, the needs of different clientele groups will have to be taken into account. The State Resource Centres, which conduct training programmes for key literacy functionaries and prepare reading materials, and other NGOs engaged in these activities need to draw inspiration from research in these areas so that the material prepared by them and the training conducted by them lead to improvements in programme implementation.

In the field of education, there is a tremendous explosion of knowledge, but we have not succeeded in uniformly meeting our needs for achieving world class standards. Quality education is possible when it aims at the full development of the learner-the mind, the heart and the ability to act, i.e, thinking, feeling and doing. However, in our system of higher education, one of the major problems is our narrow focus on knowledge, which is not necessarily integrated or up to date, and the exclusion of development of skills/attitudes and values in the learner. Another problem is the lack of stated mission for the institution, a vision of what it wishes to achieve, so that, all the activities and sub-systems, of teachers and students strive a common goal in this joint effort.

Our aim is not to produce large number of educated unemployed, but to prepare students for a career. The education system needs to be reoriented. A majority (80%) of the students terminate at the undergraduate level. Mainly these students are in humanities and social sciences (38%), commerce (22%) and life sciences (21%). The problem is how this large number of students (81%) achieves at least a minimum competence for moving into the employed market or in self employment. The need, therefore, is to make greatest impact on relevance of education to social needs at that level where bulk of our students graduate.

Development of the University

The focus should be the development of the university on the areas of: (1) Relevance of quality of education, (2) Access and equality, (3) Utility of NGOs , (4) Management of education, (5) Finance, (6) Increase the technology.

Relevance and Quality of Education

Career development for students in both undergraduate and postgraduate studies should be a major focus. Starting of vocational, application oriented courses and modifying existing traditional courses should be the major thrust. The focus has to be on making theory and practice on integral part of the subject. At least a beginning can be made by identifying one college in a district for interaction between educational institution with industry, agriculture and rural development.

Access and Equality

Due to regional imbalance, the university should pay more attention to the colleges in backward or tribal and rural areas, to bring them in the mainstream of university education. Special programme for these areas must be developed, looking into their needs, along with the programme for minorities, women and reserved categories.

Utility of NGOs

NGOs are not able to execute master plans of development. They have no commitment to the overall macro economic or macro-social structure. They intervene locally, regionally, sectorally. The problems being faced by the NGOs in carrying out their activities are many and varied. Government too is facing problems in this respect. One of the main factors responsible for their problems; was their perception. NGOs had done good work. We must emphasis the need to develop a relationship of mutual and trust. Government has to regard NGOs as equal partners in the process of development and NGOs have to operate within the constitutional and legal frame work of the country. Only then there would be better cooperation between both of them. The NGOs and private industries are the major sources of employment for the graduates and post-graduates, especially from the social sectors, like agriculture, mining, manufacturing, construction, electricity, gas and water supply, trade, transport, storage and communication services, etc.

Management of Education

Effectiveness and efficiency are requires for good management. The degree of flexibility of the institution, social and economic, is vital to its survival in changing context. In deciding the management pattern of the university it must have inbuilt flexibility to adopt itself quickly to the changing needs of the country and the region it serves, and carries out innovations and experiments. To have better coordination and interaction between the University and the State Government, other universities, UGC, HRD ministry, SCHE (state council) and NGOs must be established.

Finance

The Centre is spending less in higher education and State universities, the state's share is also not sufficient to carry out innovative programmes to have quality education. The university should, therefore, have self supporting programmes or to collaborate with NGOs and to start some programmes. It should develop a differential fee structure based on the nature of the course and socio-economic background of the students. There should be proper university-NGO collaboration for training and research support, consultancy by teachers and rending services to NGOs by the University.

Increase the Technology

Education prepares students for the use of ICT in education, further occupation and social life. Having to use of ICT in an innovative manner is an important bottleneck teachers have to cope with. It is more important that students learn how to search, select, process and use of information. To enlarge the role of the universities in the process of implementing ICT, it is suggested to stimulate a collective approach of solving problems in concrete teaching and learning situations.

Unemployment Problem

A man has to perform many roles in his life, the most crucial of which, is that of an earning member. It is crucial not because of a man spends approximately one-third of his lifetime performing this role but because it determine both livelihood and status and also enables the individual to support his family and fulfill the social obligation to the family and society. A man with a doctoral degree (Ph.D.) works as petty clerk in an office, he will not be considered as "unemployed" person, and at most, he would be viewed as "underemployed" person. An unemployed person is, "one who having potentialities and willingness to earn, but unable to find a remunerative work."

Despite the attempts of the Government, education and training have not been accessible for many in the informal sector. Apart from problems of location, disruption of regular worklife and other similar difficulties, formal education and training are not easy to access. For the poor who constitute a majority of the workforce in the informal sector, the relevant cost of education and training is not the monetary cost but the opportunity cost of discontinuing, even temporarily, their occupations of earning their livelihoods on a day-to-day basis. Unless they see a direct linkage between programmes and their own income-generating capabilities, it is rare they will preserve in acquiring education through universities.

Although there do exist training interventions by the universities for the informal sector, most skill requirements in the sector are developed through means such as traditional apprenticeship. To drive and deliver training programmes oriented to the specific skill requirements of the client group and designed to take into account the variety of social, cultural, local and political and technological factors affecting it, therefore demands a high level of expertise, combined with insight, empathy and flexibility of approach. It is largely for these reasons that NGOs have been more successful than the Government in education and training in the skilled and unemployed sector.

Responsibility of NGOs

The Government has been honest enough to acknowledge the importance of involving NGOs in the various developmental tasks of the country. As early as in the First Year Plan it was noted that NGOs would have to bear the major responsibility for organizing various activities in different fields of welfare and human development. Over the years, this recognition has increased in scope and emphasis. The Seventh Plan explicitly expressed the intention to involve NGOs in the implementation of developmental programmes, particularly in the rural areas. The period since India's independence witnessed a dramatic increase in the number of voluntary organizations. One estimate was that between 1953 and 1980 the number of NGO increased the five-fold from about 1800 to more than 8000. The actual number if NGOs in India engaged in developmental tasks, especially by way of employment generation and employment-related education and training is likely to be larger as there are a significant number of small actions operating inconspicuously in the remote parts of the country.

Case Study of NGOs

If we concentrate the case studies for dissemination and development and welfare of the Universities, some of the major studies are (i) The Behavioural Science Centre, Ahmedabad, (ii) Utthan Mahiti, Ahamedabad Study Action Group Agency, (iii) Self-Employed Women's Association, Gujarat and (iv) Shroff's Foundation Trust, Kalali Village, Baroda city.

All the activities of the studies can be broadly divided in the following areas:

1. Health services, mobile dispensary, community health, rehabilitation of malnourished children, family planning, prevention and cure of T.B and leprosy, malaria prevention programmes and combining epidemics.
2. Establishing an information network at the village level.
3. Creating community participation through formal or informal groups of local people and creating a social entrepreneurial force.
4. Achieving community confidence through demonstration and experimentation.
5. Helping of people to solve drinking water problems, saline water land development, prawn cultivation, charcoal-making, bio-gas knowledge and community health programmes.
6. Video documentation training of members for operating communication equipment, showing videos slides in the villages, making posters, pamphlets, exhibitions activities.
7. Women and child-welfare (including energy sanitation, water purification, embroidery, soap making, plumbing and roof tile making).
8. Special services such as help in emergencies like floods, free medical treatment of eligible families, and a baseline survey of about 6000 families with continuous updating of data.

Case Studies' Results of NGOs

From the four case studies of NGOs engaged in the educational approaches, which are similar but at the same time have a number of similarities which seem to represent the strategy followed by NGOs. BSC adopted a basic strategy of education for conscientization on the assumption that social awareness needs to be combined with the imparting of the basic skills of economic activity. SEWA was less concerned with matters of ideology and opted for a pragmatic approach of promoting the economic independence of women by giving them skills and other support services. Utthan Mahiti used the method of providing technical help and know-how related to the problems of the local community. The SFT's approach is characteristic of the approach followed by agencies supported and promoted by philanthropic business houses in India, that of welfare dispensation and service oriented activity.

NGOs clearly have an important role to play and involve in educational field and training for self-employment among marginal and underprivileged groups. By using a community-based approach to development, the NGOs also help build a social support structure which enables a certain amount of economic risk-taking which would otherwise be impossible for the poor who have little or no capacity for risk-taking.

Conclusion

However, as a rule, NGOs in a country like India may not be able to contribute adequately to education and training for non-traditional, individual self-employment. Such education and training, to have an impact, requires large scale investments in infrastructure and institution building. NGOs may be neither ideologically included toward such activity nor have the resources for it. This will remain a task which the Government and formal sector institutions like Universities must continue to perform.

REFERENCES

1. Noorjahan Bava., (1997) *Non-Governmental Organisations in Development*, Kanishka Pub, New Delhi. pp. 209-211.
2. Nachimuthu, K et al (1990) *Enrolment and Employment in Higher Education*, International Educator, Thiruvananthapuram, Kerala.
3. Sareen, N (2005), *Information and Communication Technology*, Anmol Pub. Pvt. Ltd., New Delhi, p. 332.

2

Problems and Prospects of University-NGO Partnership

NGOs Point of View

Prof. M.C. Reddeppa Reddy
Sri D. Ramakrishna

Introduction

Sri Venkateswara University, Tirupati has shown interest to have a much closer partnership with civil society organisations, industries, community, non-governmental organisations, etc. to improve the effectiveness and efficiency of the educational programs. University is of the opinion that the above organisations/institutions are serving the rural communities and also providing employment opportunities for its students. But, the NGOs are feeling that the students who are coming out of the Universities are not tuned/oriented to meet the requirements of the organisations. Most of the students do not have good aptitude to work in the rural areas and they do not possess sufficient competencies and skills to carryout their work in social service activities. However, the chief functionaries of NGO organisations are expecting much from Universities and are ready to use the services of staff and [illegible] in the voluntary sector. An attempt has been made to [illegible] with the chief functionaries on the various issues [illegible] and presented in this chapter.

Objectives of the Brain Storming

A brain storming session was conducted with the following objectives:

(a) To know about the NGO collaboration with other institutions/organisations.

(b) To understand the problems in employing the college students in social work activities.

(c) To know about their expect, from the University teachers and students and how they utilise the services of students and teachers.

(d) To elicit their contributions for the college/university education; and elicit suggestions to overcome those problems.

(e) To know the expected changes to be brought in collaboration of universities with NGOs.

Methodology

A Brainstorming session was conducted with 30 NGO functionaries, 20 Chief Functionaries and 10 Programme Coordinators who met on 28th and 29th November, 2005 at Madhu Lodge, Srikalahasthi in connection with START programme organized by the IIEKS, Chennai. The purpose of session was explained and requested them to give their perceptions, problems and perspectives on the University-NGO interaction. Various questions are proposed for their reaction and noted down carefully. The questions which are posed for discussion are given hereunder.

(a) Do you have collaboration with any other organizations, and type of collaboration with them?

(b) Do you have any collaboration with local College/University, and type of collaboration with them?

(c) What roles do you expect from the College/University teachers and students?

(d) What way do you utilise the services of the College/University teachers and students?

(e) How do you (as NGO) contribute for the college/ university?

(g) What problems do you have in recruiting the college students and offer suggestions to overcome those problems?

(h) What type of changes do you expect in collaboration of University with NGO?

(i) What suggestions do you offer for better collaboration between NGO and the University?

Deliberations of the Brainstorming

The deliberations on each of the questions posed to the chief functionaries are presented hereunder while presenting the outcome priority was given to the points, which were highlighted by the participants.

(a) Type of Collaboration with other NGOs

For the question posed by the researcher, i.e. Did you have collaboration with any other organisation and type of collaboration with them? Most of the participants said that they have collaboration with other NGOs and they are involved in networking, programme planning and training the functionaries, etc. They are also collaborating in the activities such as evaluation, exchange programmes and advocacy.

(b) Collaboration of NGOs with Colleges/Universities

For the question—Did you have any collaboration with the local college/university and what type of collaboration with them? Half of them said that they have collaboration with the local college/university. The responses of the participants for the type of collaboration they have are enumerated hereunder based on their frequency.

1. Exposure visits to students
2. Use of teachers services
3. Use of infrastructure facilities
4. Use of students resources
5. Sharing of experiences

(c) Expected Roles of Teachers and Students

For the question—What roles do you expect from the college/University teachers and student? the participants responded as follows:

- Expected roles of University teachers
  - (a) Act as trainer of the training programme
  - (b) Act as facilitator of the programmes/projects
  - (c) Change agents at the grassroot level
  - (d) Evaluator of the project(s)performance and outcomes
  - (e) To be the Technical consultants.
- Expected roles of the students
  - (a) Motivation and mobilization
  - (b) Work as social workers/volunteers
  - (c) Involve in surveys as investigators
  - (d) Act as change agents
  - (e) Documentation and material development

(d) Utilisation of Teachers and Students by the NGOs

For the question—What way do you utilise the services of the teachers and students in their organisations? The participants responded as follows:

- Use of services of the students
  - (a) In social campaigns and awareness programmes
  - (b) Conduct of simple surveys
  - (c) To undertake simple projects/research studies
  - (d) Part-time volunteers or social workers.
- Use of the sevices of teachers
  - (a) Formation of projects
  - (b) In conducting evaluation and research studies
  - (c) For proposal writing and report writing

(d) In nominating them on their boards/executive bodies

(e) To act as trainer or resource person

(f) In documentation work.

(e) Contributions of NGOs to the University

For the question— How do you contribute for the college/ university? the participants responded in the following manner:

(a) Providing field exposure to students

(b) Providing apprenticeship and internship training for the students

(c) Selecting the students for social service

(d) Serving on the board of studies

(e) Acting as Adjunct Professors in training the students.

(f) Problems in Recruiting the Students

For the question— the type of problems that they are facing in recruiting the college students, they said that:

(a) Lack of commitment towards the social service

(b) Lack of field orientation and experience

(c) Lack of tact and poor communication skills

(d) High expectations of salary and job

(e) No interest to work in rural communities

(f) Poor understanding and capabilities.

(g) The suggestions that they offer to overcome the problems with the Students

(a) Organise internship and apprenticeship training with NGOs

(b) Developing aptitude towards social service

(c) Imparting communication skills

(d) Providing field orientation

(e) Organise exposure visits

(f) Assign simple field projects.

(h) Expected changes to be brought in Collaboration of University-NGO

For the question— What type of changes do you expect in collaboration of University with NGO? The participants said that:

(a) Develop the capabilities and skills of the students

(b) Enhance confidence and trust on the NGOs among the communities

(c) Sustainability of projects/programmes

(d) Improve the quality of projects/services organised by NGOs

(e) Find solutions to the critical problems

(f) Universities would become preaching and practice centres

(g) Quick transformation of rural areas

(h) Capacity building for the NGOs.

(i) Suggestions for Better Collaboration

For the question— What suggestions do you offer for better collaboration between NGO and the College/University? They offer the following suggestions:

(a) Organising periodic interaction with the University

(b) Launching joint activities/projects

(c) Appointing the teachers on the boards of organisations and vice-versa

(d) Developing a plan of action for University-NGO interaction

(e) Entering an MU with the University/NGO

(f) Acting the university as pre-active leader

(g) Creating a coordination committee for better collaboration.

Conclusion

Universities are no longer the ivory towers of learning. They have to adopt drastic reforms in order to make their students more effective and efficient for which the practice oriented education have to be offered. They come out from the examination-centre approach and adopt community-centred approach. It is known fact that the Universities are still not ready to accept the responsibility of community development under the third dimension of extension. The NGO partners should also realise their goal at helping the people to help themselves by mobilising their own resources, taping the potential of other stakeholders in finding solutions to the community problems and implementing suitable development programmes collaboratively. Let us hope for better collaboration among the develoment stakeholders for better results.

3

University and NGOs

Certain Interventions

Dr. T. Kumaraswamy
Dr. K.G. Bharathi
G. Eswaraiah

Universities as power houses of knowledge can no longer remain isolated from the community. They have to shoulder the responsibility of serving the community along with the public and private organisations. Though the educational institutions are emerging from the community, yet they are not able to change to suit the requirements of the community. They are remaining simply as centres for creation of educated unemployed with their traditional teaching and research. Universities as temples of higher learning should take initiatives to revamp their system of functioning. They should prepare students with adequate knowledge and skills to become employed in the NGO sector which is having a lot of opportunities. Today, the society requires not merely graduates of engineering or medicine, but those who can help the community to overcome the wide range of problems like poverty, illiteracy, ill health, bonded labour etc. The present paper tries to focus on the interventions needed for promoting the NGO sector.

There are different development programmes and initiatives taken up by the voluntary agencies to improve the quality of life of rural masses. These programmes/activities are related to housing schemes, drinking water, land development, water sheds, tree plantation, literacy, primary education, family planning, tribal development, sericulture, health expects, etc.

The prominent areas in which the NGOs have already made valuable contributions are as follows:

(a) Actually playing a leadership and supportive role (in collaboration with the government) in operationalising decentralized planning with people's participation, e.g., Kerala Sastra Sahitya Parishat (KSSP), Kerala;

(b) Developing and popularisng the participatory learning and planning methods and approaches, e.g., Mysore Relief and Development Agency (MYRADA), Karnataka;

(c) Creating cadre of professionals who are equipped with the knowledge, skills and sensitivities to take up leadership roles in operationalising multi-level decentralized planning, e.g., Centre for Development Studies and Activities (CDSA), Pune, Maharashtra;"

(d) Developing and implementing innovative and replicable grassroots development models, e.g., Pani Panchayat, Maharashtra; and

(e) Cost-effective and efficient delivery of services and resource mobilization for local level development initiatives, e.g., Bharatiya Agro Industries Foundation (BAIF), Pune, Maharashtra.

The names of agencies mentioned above are given only for illustrative purposes. There are many more worthy examples of NGOs specializing and contributing in similar ways across the country. For example, Mysore Relief and Development Agency (MYRADA) is one of the highly successful NGOs in India and was established in 1968 as an organization which resettled refugees from Tibet. Currently it is working in over 2,000 villages in the states of Andhra Pradesh, Karnataka and Tamil Nadu. MYRADA offers some significant grassroots development programmes. They emphasise on developing and popularizing participatory learning and planning methods.

Working with the Government

MYRADA has adopted a three-pronged strategy in order to foster the process of change and influence public policies in favour of the poor. They are as follows:

- To target the system for structural change in the long run, and for the creation and implementation of new policies and legislation in favour of the poor in the medium term;
- To support relevant components in the system and responsive officials in implementing government programmes and policies to eradicate poverty; and
- To support the emergence of alternative innovative and appropriating institutions of the people in their efforts towards self-reliance.

The contribution of MYRADA has been remarkable in popularising Participatory Learning Methods (PALM). It has given to the state government bureaucrats in PALM which is said to be very effective in changing the latter's attitude towards effective micro-level participatory planning and programme implementation with people's participation. PRA has reportedly engendered a qualitative change in the attitudes of the people, government and NGO functionaries and that is reflected in the following outcomes:

- Raised awareness and self-confidence leading to greater willingness among villagers to act without outside financial support;
- Increased devolution of responsibility from implementing agencies to rural people themselves;
- Raised local awareness resulting in increased local monitoring;
- Improved capabilities in NGO and government staff;
- Breakdown of barriers within villages, between government and villages, and between government departments;

- More sustainable watershed protection at lower cost;
- Improved monitoring through the use of villages' maps.

Opportunities are available for students in the NGO sector to work as area managers/promoters/office managers/specialists in micro-finance. Here the NGOs require competencies/abilities relating to establishment of bank linkages, organising the self-help groups to form into associations, monitoring the programmes of self-help groups, ability to prepare the budget requirements, ability to establish rapport with development agencies, business partnerships, skills in preparing documents, project proposals and training modules and skills in operating. computer. They also expect the perspective candidates to be good at communication skills, organization of training programmes, group discussions, etc. Hence, the Universities and colleges should modify their course structure at the degree or post-graduation level to equip the students on the above lines.

Avenues are available for students in development projects like Velugu, District Rural Development Agency. Here students are selected for positions like community co-ordinators, livelihood associates, district resource persons etc. Apart from looking into the general qualifications of candidates, the agencies are looking into the competencies like concern for the work where one anticipates and responds to the feelings, needs and concerns of others; strategic influencing where the individual is having awareness of different options and the ability to select the appropriate options, Le., the skill of decision-making; initiative to seize the opportunities to bring in changes in direction, policy and to proactively scan the environment for new ideas, trends, etc., inter-personal awareness where the individual is expected to sense the ideas, moods, concerns, interests, feelings and emotions of others; tenacity which refers to the individual's ability to make repeated and enduring efforts to overcome obstacles with a plan of action until the objective is achieved; patience to continuously perform effectively in stressful and difficult situations; critical information seeking where the individual gathers critical information from individua'ls, offices and key sources; development orientation which refers to the individuals efficiency to identify and provide appropriate opportunities or training to improve the capabilities of other people; and consensus building which refers to the ability of the individual to facilitate the community to become independent and self-reliant. The universities and colleges are expected to improve the knowledge and skills of the students to fit into poverty reduction initiative programmes. The students require self-managing abilities to work with the poorest of the poor, influencing skills and achievement orientation to continue in the projects. The students should also be trained in conducting survey relating to microplanning, organisation of discussions, preparation of consolidated reports, etc. Exposure of this nature would be of immense help to the students during the recruitment process. The universities have to take up measures to introduce vocational courses at the graduate level as a separate or in-built scheme with the degree courses. If the students are possessing vocational skills or skills in different trades like motor winding, radio repair, TV mechanism, computer repair, first aid, etc., there is a greater possibility for them to survive either independently or at NGO level. The greatest thing that is missing in the educational sector is lack of proper manpower planning. We are producing millions of graduates to suit the clerical positions for which opportunities are rare.

NGOs are growing quantitatively at local, district, state, national and international levels. The main problem with them is lack of continuity and perpetual existence. The reasons are many like lack of continuous financial support, lack of clarity in objectives, lack of trained staff, lack of proper management, lack of proper incentives to workers, lack of co-ordination with others, one man show, lack of records, reports, etc. Some of the NGOs cannot be found even at the addresses given. Some of the NGOs are handled by external agencies and after exhausting finances or due to corruption activities from public they turn back their boards. Some of the NGOs continue with court activities. Some of the NGOs work for political parties or vested interests, whereas some NGOs maintain cordial relations with financing agencies without doing work. There is a need for intervention of the universities to conduct research on the status, problems, activities of NGOs to provide clear position for the various agencies. In some cases some reputed agencies take the benefit of all activities, leaving nothing to other NGOs. Here, the process of co-ordination, facilitation may be taken by the universities through workshops, discussions, etc. Capacity building or training of NGOs may be taken up by the universities keeping in view their requirements and demands. Universities have the infrastructural facilities like library, laboratories, academicians and experts representing different departments like law, human rights, home science, population studies. They can provide exposure to different extension training methods like role play, group discussion, brainstorming, etc., to members of NGOs to suit to their positions. Documentation of the different activities of NGOs is yet another important one where the universities can pay attention. Though there are journals in English, still there is a greater need for journals published in the regional languages and the universities may taken such activity for the benefit of students teachers and various organizations. Let the universities and NGOs collaboration open new avenues and facilities and let this collaboration herald, symbolise and contribute to new development strategies.

REFERENCES

Venkat Ravi, R., Narayana Reddy, V., Venkataramana, M. (2004), *Empowerment of People*, Kanishka Publishers, Distributors, New Delhi.

Khanka, S.S. (2002) "*Entrepreneurial Development*", S. Chand & Company Ltd., Ram Nagar, New Delhi-110 055.

4

Linkage between Universities and Non-Governmental Organisations:

Present Status and Future Directions

Prof. N. Venkataiah

Present Status

The Non-governmental organizations involved creating infrastructure, implementing programmes and contributing for the human resource development in their humble way. The efforts of the NGO's have yet to be maximized to meet the requirements of our vast and populous country.

The Universities are producing innumerable graduates, postgraduates, doctorates and diploma holders every year. These human resources have to be utilized by the society. The NGOs and private industries are the major sources of employment for the graduates and postgraduates especially from social sciences. But they are not able to utilize the manpower from-the universities directly due to lack of required skills among these graduates. There is a wide gap between the skills possessed by the graduates and skills required by the agencies providing employment. Therefore there is an immediate need to bridge the gap between the resources generated by our traditional universities and the resources required by the NGOs so as to utilize the human resources directly by the NGOs and industries.

As this chapter deals with the linkage to be established exclusively between universities and NGOs, let us go through a brief report on a well known NGO—M.V. Foundation.

M. V. Foundation

Mamidipudi Venkatarangaiya foundation or MV Foundation, which has its base in the Ranga Reddy District of the State of Andhra Pradesh in South India has developed a unique and powerful approach to deal with the twin problems of child labour and illiteracy. Starting in a small way in 1991, it has grown into a complex organizations employing a wide range of strategies.

At the core of MV Foundations strategy for transforming children from labourers to students are the bridge camps. These are residential camps where children who have never been to school are prepared to enter the formal school system in classes appropriate to their age. The bridge course has emerged as a very successful strategy for older children to be mainstreamed into regular schools.

M.V. Foundation has been very active in assisting and training NGOs across the country to replicate its programme strategies. UNDP is supporting a project with MVF as a national resource center for the campaign to get children out of work and into schools. Dr. Shantha Sinha, the moving spirit behind MVF was given the Megsaysay Award in 2003.

The major work of the Universities is conducting research and teaching. The third dimension of the university viz., extension work is very megre or negligible. There are Extension Departments like Adult and Continuing Education, Education, Population Studies and Home Science in the traditional universities. But they confine their extension activities only connected/related to the subjects concerned. Adult and Continuing Education deals with the extension activities related exclusively to Adult Education, Department of Education caters to the needs of the teacher educators through its extension activities; Population Studies deals with demographic issues and Home Science deals with the extension work of food and nutrition. The Agricultural University and Agricultural Colleges are concentrating on agricultural aspects through their extension activities. The NGOs do not usually resort to the help of the neighbouring university with the feeling the university still remain as an ivory tower does not coop up with the requirements and does not extend its helping hands to serve their needs. It is a fact that many Universities are getting satisfied with teaching and research, neglecting extension work.

Days have completely changed and now the universities should cooperate and coordinate with the welfare programmes of the community in contributing for the human resource development. The University Extension Departments should make an intensive study of the objectives and activities run by the NGOs to develop expert knowledge.

The objectives and activities of 5 NGOs which are selected randomly are given here for a better understanding of the work of NGOs.

1. Dr. Ambedkar Dalitha Varga Abhivruddi Sangam, Masapet, Cuddapah District, Andhra Pradesh

Main Objectives

(1) To raise literacy levels of poor people by providing them easy access to educational facilities, (2) To run income generating programmes for girls and women, and (3) To establish vocational training centers for skill development.

Main Activities

(1) Running a girls hostel under the MHRD scheme of strengthening boarding and lodging facilities for girls at the high secondary stage, (2) Imparting training to girls and women in various vocational skills such as typing, computer literacy etc. (3) Organizing training programmes, workshops, campaigns and extension programmes for promotion of girls) education and (4) Mobilizing masses by conducting public awareness campaigns for enrolling the girl children in schools.

2. Andhra Mahila Sabha, Hyderabad

Main Objectives

(1) To Promote education particularly among women, (2) To impart training in arts, crafts and other vocations, (3) To provide facilities for physical training, games and sports for

women, (4) To produce and publish materials addressing issues relating to education and social welfare, and (5) To supplement development and welfare schemes of government.

Main Activities

Running a number of centers/institutions such as: (1) Mahila Vidyalaya aiming at catering to the educational needs of girls whose parents get transferred to the city, school drop-outs, late starters and slow learners, (2) Ashraya (Integrated shelter project) Providing shelter and skill development training to girls and women in distress, (3) Preparing girls for the high school examination, and (4) Conducting vocational Job-oriented) courses for girls and women. Apart from this, organization is also running colleges, hospitals and legal aid centers for women etc.

3. Krishna Sai Education Society, Guntur (A.P.)

Main Objectives

(1) To promote education in the society with emphasis on gender equality, (2) To provide educational opportunities to those children, particularly girls, belonging to weaker sections of the society and (3) To conduct surveys and undertake research project in the filed of education.

Main Activities

(1) Running a junior college in the rural area of Bhattiprolu block of Guntur district to enable girls to continue their higher studies, (2) Running a girl's hostel under the MHRD scheme of boarding and lodging facilities for girls and study centers for educationally week students, (3) Introducing thrift and credit activities through self-help groups (SHGs), (4) Running occupational training programmes of one month duration for girls such as tailoring, computer literacy and weaving, and (5) Developing motivational and publicity materials in the form of leaflets and news letter related to the different aspects of girls' education.

4. Center for Health Education Training and Nutrition Awareness, Ahmadabad, Gujarat State

Main Objectives

To empower adolescent girls and boys; disadvantaged women and children to enable them to gain control over their own, their families and communities health.

Main Activities

(1) Provide health and nutrition education to girls and women, (2) Running early Childcare and Education Centers for 6 years children, (3) Capacity building for organization through Training of Train (TOT), (4) Documenting experiences developing disseminating need-based e1J.vcation and. training materials and net working, and advocating the concerns vulnerable groups, (5) Development of print and electronic materials on issues of gender awareness and gender integration in the health sector.

5. C.P. Ramaswami Aiyar Foundation, Alwarpet, Chennai.

Main Objectives

(1) To improve the socio-economic and lifestyles of diverse people through education.

Main Activities

(1) To undertake Research studies and conduct surveys concerning women, (2) Organise seminars and symposia on women's issues and (3) Providing training in a variety of vocational skills for women, such as, craft skills and entrepreneurship skills, thus empowering women—(a) organize women craft bazaar to facilitate women's entrepreneurs to market their product, (b) Train women in traditional tribal art forms, (c) The foundation is educating 126 girls from classes VI-X in a local high school belonging to women headed families and have arranged individual sponsors for each child (d). Running skill training centers for adolescent girls in traditional drawings and painting (e) Organise women's cricket camps for school girls, (f) Help women in learning to identify hubs and prepare home remedies with locally available herbs,

(g) Foundation has set up Saraswathi Kendra Learning Center (innovative center) for children. The center provides those supplements necessary for the all-round development of the child, girls are the main beneficiaries of this center.

NGOs have diverse objectives and activities. They differ from one NGO to another. A careful observation of these five NGO's objectives and activities enable any one to arrive at a conclusion that providing educational facilities for the people in the community is a very important objective of all NGOs. The NGOs mainly concentrate on Raising literacy level particularly among girls and women (Elementary Education), Providing Adult Literacy and Continuing Education and Running income generating programmes including vocational training for skill development.

Elementary Education

The University Department of Education must. be well equipped with the growing knowledge and developments taking place in the primary education to cater to the needs of the NGOs who provide educational facilities to raise literacy level among the people in the community.

Universalisation of Elementary Education

The Programmes that are being implemented for Universalization of Elementary Education and equity are as follows:

1. Sarva Shiksha Abhiyan (SSA)
2. National Programme for Education of Girls at Elementary Level (NPEGEL)

Sarva Shiksha Abhiyan

The SSA Programme purpose is Universal Elementary Education (UEE) with adequate facilities for 8 years of elementary schooling of satisfactory quality and provision of alternative schooling facilities in unserved habitations, effective pedagogical interventions to make school attractive, and provision of adequate and context specific initiatives to promote equality by specially targeting the most deprived children.

Objectives of SSA

The Objectives of SSA are as follows:

1. All Children of school age should be back to school campus by 2003
2. Ensure that all children complete 5 years of primary schooling by 2007
3. Ensure that all children complete years elementary schooling by 2010
4. Provide elementary education of satisfactory quality with emphasis on education for life
5. Bridge all gender and social category gaps at primary stage by 2007 and at elementary level by 2010 and
6. Universal retention by 2010.

Quality Improvement Initiatives

The quality improvement initiatives include capacity development of teachers, making the academic support system, effective canalysing evaluation outcomes and focus on remedial measures and through intensive monitoring which will focus on school improvement.

1. Teacher Development

The teacher is the key factor to facilitate the academic inputs in schools.

(a) Training of untrained teachers

(b) Inservice Training: In service trainings have to be organized for teachers whose capacities need to be enhanced. It should be need-based training. This training is only given to week and needy teachers. The content of training is to be decided on the basis of training needs of teachers. Training needs have to be identified through various tools like learners' evaluation analysis, school monitoring and discussion with teachers in monthly meetings etc. The broad areas/topics to be covered in the inservice training programme are as follows: (1) Assessed learning difficulties and hard abstract areas in subject content, (2) Pedagogical issues, (3) Evaluation techniques and (4) Educational planning and management at school level.

(c) Induction Training

Newly recruited teachers have to be given induction training at least for 20 days. The context of induction training at primary level is as follows: (1) Basic subject context—Telugu, Maths, Environment Science and English, (2)Teaching Process, (3) Evaluation Technique and (4) Planning and Management.

2. Learner Evaluation

Evaluation of learning-achievement is the most critical activity as it reflects the overall impact of initiatives for quality improvement. The learner evaluation system is to be improved to make it non-threatening, competency-based and designed to provide a basis for diagnostic and remedial teaching. Monthly quarterly and annual tests are to be conducted to determine the promotion of learner to higher grades. The monthly, quarterly and annual tests are followed by analysis of the answer sheets of his learner to identify the hand spots and difficulties faced by the learner. This becomes the base for formulation of remedial measures, which is decided by the teacher in consultation with the University Department and accordingly in interventions are planned. Students are provided with grades based on the percentage of marks they obtain.

3. The Training Plan

1. Long Term Training—9 months
2. Training for teachers in subjects—10 days—Telugu, Mathematics, Environmental Science and English
3. Refresher training for primary level teachers—20 days
4. Short term training—3 days
5. Skill development training—5 days
6. Preparation of resource material—Preparation of audio cassette in workshop mode for primary level

Bridge Course

Bridge course are started with the objective of mainstreaming the overage-out-of-school children into the schools. Two types of bridge-courses, residential and nonresidential bridge course is run for ensuring that all overage out-of-school children are targeted and mainstreamed into the formal schools.

Residential Bridge Course

Residential bridge course is started for those children who need to be taken away from the environment, which prevents them to attend school and bridge course. These are the working children, child labour, children of economically disadvantaged families, children of parents involved in unsocial activities urban derived children etc.

Non-residential Bridge Course (in identified habitations/ villages)

The non-residential bridge courses will run for at least 20 out-of-school (never enrolled/dropout) per course. In specific remote/tribal area the number of children could be 15. The out-of-school children will be identified by the teacher of every school. The teacher will prepare a list of out-of-school children and submit it to the NGO. Bridge course class will be conducted in close proximity of the school. In specific conditions where sufficient space is not available in the community will provide space. The place will not be very far from the school.

Adult Education

The University Department of Adult and Continuing Education should be familiar with the knowledge in adult literacy and continuing education and other aspects of adult education.

Evaluation Studies

Evaluation has a major role to play in strengthening the literacy campaign by identifying the merits and demerits of the programme. Its major functions are:

1. To cover the dropouts, absentees and newly attained age groups remaining illiterate

2. To enable district to propose new and innovative strategies to maximize the performance in the literacy efforts
3. To evaluate different strategies to be adopted in (1) environment building, motivation of learners, (2) teaching learning materials, (3) training of volunteers, (4) impact of the campaigns, (5) attitude of learners, (6) achievement of learners in literacy skills, and (7) problems of learners in attending the centers.

The studies conducted by the Department of Adult Education offer workable solutions to improve the programme (campaign) mainly from three important angles viz., (a) environment building, motivation of 1earners, (b) teaching learning materials and (c) training volunteers and (d) impact of the campaigns.

Adult education has more significant influence on industrial workers and the manufacturing sector because the pace of technological change and innovations are much faster, more pronounced manufacturing than in agriculture.

Evaluation reports on various aspects of National Adult Education Programme indicate the following:

1. The learning environment was found to be lacking in basic amenities conducive to learning.
2. Functionaries, particularly instructors were not properly trained.
3. Learner's motivation was low, attendance rate was low and dropout rate was high.
4. While many reported learning the 3 R's, functionality and social awareness were not adequately covered.
5. There was no effective mechanism for post-literacy efforts to sustain what has been learned.
6. Bureaucratic procedures made administrative support particularly for voluntary agencies, difficult and there was considerable misreporting about centers and their functioning.

7. Participation and motivation of women and SC/ST learners was high and the programme seemed to have done well in those states where functionaries were more committed to the programme.

Kumaraswamy (2005) identified the problems of learners of the total literacy campaigns as follows:

1. Personal problems
2. Social/Community based problems
3. Economic Problem
4. Programme related problems

The Department of Adult and Continuing Education should find suitable/appropriate solutions to all the problems and suggest NGOs to implement them while conducting Adult Education Programmes.

Continuing Education

Under the programme of continuing education, activities are conducted for neo-literates. This provides an opportunity for generating awareness towards elementary education. The rural libraries set up under continuing education are also catering to the children in age group (10-14 years) also. These children can participate in the activities conducted for neo-literates and share resources like library, games and sports etc. The preraks at the village level are animators for adult and elementary education. The preraks are part of facilitator groups and are also involved in school activities and for helping dropout children to continue their education.

Research and Evaluation

Research and evaluation studies are considered as an in-built component of the programme. Research studies help in understanding the issues and problems in the implementation of programme and suggesting solutions to the identified problems.

Research and evaluation studies will be conducted to assess the needs so as to plan and implement appropriate strategies. In addition to concurrent and impact studies will be conducted to assess the impact of various inputs on the educational outcomes will also be taken up by the NGOs under the guidance of University Departments to develop better understanding on the classroom processes and seek remedial measures for learning-difficulties and difficult areas faced by the students and teachers.

Research studies on the following topics may be conducted:

1. A study on the role of PT A in the school improvement programme
2. A study of pupil evaluation procedure and practices, sharing the pupils progress cards with parent and the use of evaluation outcomes as feedback to improve teaching learning process.
3. Impact of assessment of community participation on civil works.
4. A study to find the disparity that exists in enrolment and attendance of boys and girls.

The selected functionaries of NGOs will be provided with training on different aspects of research. The capacity building of functionaries will improve the quality of research.

Future Directions

1. The Ministry of Human Resource Development has to order Universities through the University Grants Commission that they should extend their human resources for the successful conduct of the activities run by the NGOs. The NGOs also have to establish linkage with the Universities and utilize their expertise maximally for the successful conduct of welfare and educational programmes run by them.
2. The Ministry of Human Resource Development should direct the Universities to help the NGOs free of cost as a matter of responsibility and social-service.
3. One of the major tasks of NGOs would be to ensure that all the children of school going age are enrolled in school and are regular in attending the school.

4. Any parent/guardian, if found guilty of not sending or preventing children to go to school is punishable will be liable to pay fine as declared by the District Collector.
5. The Extension Departments of the Universities which will help the NGOs and with whom the NGOs have to establish linkage, should know in detail all their activities curricula of different programmes/ courses. The Extension Departments should have a comprehensive understanding and in-depth knowledge of the programmes of the NGOs.
6. The MHRD should identify the NGOs and University Departments with whom the NGOs have to develop linkage. It is better to have linkage between the NGO and the near by University to enable better interactions and consultation is possible.
7. The University Departments with which the NGOs establish linkage should know in detail the objectives and activates of the NGOs and equip themselves with expert knowledge to assist the NGOs.

5

Linkages between NGOs and Universities

Status and Future Strategies

Dr. N. Jayakumar Rao

Dr. D.S. Kothari while submitting a report of the Education Commission to Govt. of India has mentioned that education of the yester years may not fulfil the needs of today and the present education may not fulfil the needs of tomorrow. He said, that this strategies of education and its priorities should change with the changing needs of the society. NGOs and Universities must help mutually for substantial enhancement, and capacity building. The NGOs have practical knowledge of the issues related to Management and Administration of the work they are involved in. The universities have with them a treasure and wealth of theoretical methodology with which the human resources are produced. The universities have, some time ago, introduced a dash of practicality into the curricula, but not adequately. If this gap can be bridged, the benefits are innumerable. Just as the laboratories are the avenues for experiments in pure sciences, so are the NGOs in Social Sciences. The university methods of working with groups and communities should be field-tested with the NGOs. The existing methodologies are excellent, but that alone does not suffice, when the qualified Human Resources get to brass tracks with the voluntary organizations. I am sure that conferences or seminars of this nature will enormously help build the development of interdependence.

Potentialities

The institutions of higher learning are considered the centres for knowledge, expertise and resources. They must be made available to the community around to solve its problems. The two streams, once they begin to work hand in hand, would upgrade the holistic partnership. The one works for theoretical research orientation, the other partakes in the action research. If the working strategies of both are integrated, both will reap the rich fruit of it. After all, education should lead the society towards all-round advancement. If this integration and interdependence are not given due significance, the existing gap is sure to become a gulf, and the Human Resources of universities will never be useful to the NGOs, Industries or Government agencies. The NGOs and Industries are in constant touch with the needs of community. If the University diamonds are kept at a decent distance from the common man's consumption, of what earthly use are the diamonds. If the scholastic potentialities of the books and methodologies of the universities are not tailored to suit the requirements of both the entities, employment of the human resources remains only a dream. This is possible only through the participation of Teachers and students in extension services. There should be a continuous interaction and involvement between the students, college and community.

I think, that at this stage, I should enumerate some of my personal experiences as one associated with many NGOs. Just an advertisement in any leading news daily brings loads of applications for jobs. After screening the applications and sending interview call letters, the NGOs appoint a committee to interview and select the best five among the screened fifty. I happened to be on several such Interviewing Committees and had the good fortune of interacting with the highly qualified University products.

Let us say the NGO is working on social issues pertaining to drug abuse, AIDS, Leprosy, Street Children, prostitution, the physically, mentally or visually handicapped, the child labour, general health and education projects, the polio-affected, the community development of fishermen or rehabilitation of farmers families whose heads committed suicide, the families of long-term sentenced prisoners, child-care, care for the aged or those who are in distress, those who are underprivileged social segments like tribals, illiterate villagers, slum dwellers in urban setup, disaster relief in nature calamities, irrigation, drinking water, adult and continuing education, Oh! the list is inexhaustible in our developing nation. The industries may be dealing with their own products.

Now, begins the avalanche of questions. Not one among the 50 has any practical knowledge of the issues above. He does not know what voluntary work actually is. "What are the various intricacies, implications and complications involved in tackling this or that problem, which this NGO is dealing with?" The candidate, with all his big bunch of certificates, begins to blink sweet ignorance of any of these bitter social issues. My question to the university Human Resources is, "What have you been doing in these years of studying social sciences?" Pat comes the response, "Sir, ask me about the theory. Unless I work with an NGO, how do you expect me to speak of the practical problems. Give me a chance to work. I shall learn" and as the misfortune would have it, the NGO has already some personnel wrestling with the problems of the project. But it realised that it is working unscientifically. What they want is somebody who is well qualified to rescue their organisation from the problems creeping in, with immediate effect. Not somebody whom they will now initiate and induct to acquire training. It means waste of time, energy and money. Eventually, these inadequately trained person but bestowed with a fund of theoretical knowledge, will create a new set of complications and headaches, created because of his insufficient field exposure. I am speaking of field knowledge, not of wisdom, which is quite another subject that has no bearing on the topic on hand.

The Linkage

Yes, this is what is miserably missing. The NGOs have the money. What they do not have, is personnel who can efficiently handle their issues and the annoying sub-complications of the main issues. After all, problems are the integral part of any living organisation, be it an *NGO* or an Industry or a Government Agency. And management is solving problems. After solving today's problems, there will be fresh problems the next morning. Nobody is an Almighty God to solve all the problems of Government, Non-Government Organisations or Industries. But we expect basic practical knowledge from the Human Resource we employ. There will be specialists to deal with special problems. I am speaking of fundamental knowledge of practical problems on the part of University Human Resource. The institutions of higher learning should take proper care and interest in preparing the students and teachers to take up community development programs in their own areas of specialization. Not that they are not doing it now, but only that it is not adequate.

Short-comings of NGOs

1. In most of the cases, the monetary emoluments given to their personnel are too low to take care of the employees' own financial problems.
2. Some NGOs are afraid that the university products will interfere with the management. What they want is intervention and what they get is interference.
3. The job guarantee and perks are deplorably poor, so much so, the personnel are under constant fear of being fired after being hired. I am speaking of the job-insecurity.
4. Some NGOs, for reasons of ignorance of Government rules and regulations related to their own work, expect the university products to solve their problems, on an emergency basis. That leads to emergence of other problems. Then again, the lack of will in the employee to put in hard work. This is detriment to the progress of the NGO, as against the promotion of their aims and objectives. So, they are forced to seek help from experts and professionals for solutions to their problems. Which means money again. And they may not be able to afford it. They

feel depressed because the University Human Resources have not solved their issues as much as they expected.

Uniting Both the Streams

If they work in partnership, NGOs must be invited for guest lectures in the Universities to share their experiences with Human Resources. Professors and students must visit the NGOs. Not just for an eyewash, to satisfy a curriculum requirement. It must be at regular intervals, with commitment and dedication. A mutual trust has to be built up. If a postgraduate does not know how to prepare a Project Proposal with an appeal for funds or with the presentation of the particular NGO he is working with, he will be irrelevant for that NGO. Employing and training him is a drain on their funds. All said and done. Science is science. An NGO that does not work with scientific awareness, will not last long. Its work will be superficial. It decays gradually, stinks periodically and disappears finally.

Curricula

It is my strong feeling that the present curricula in respect of all the departments in the University should be community-oriented. There must be extension programs and enough slots of time should be allotted for the students to work with the NGOs, Government agencies and Industries. The syllabus makers should give some serious thought to this proposition. The syllabus should take into consideration not only the study of the problems, but design programs for the effective development of the educational institutions. A capsule containing the knowledge required, and the skills needed, should be developed as the integral part of syllabus for each course of study. The programs like NSS are being implemented successfully to reach this goal, but it is too short a period of time. Further, The NGO's should also be involved in this process as link agencies and catalystic agents. The NGO's should also be given proper orientation by inviting them to series of lectures in the universities and for the needed knowledge inputs. Universities should promote debates, discussions and participations among the various agencies. The social trinity is "school students and community". They should interact with each other and work together in the development process.

Epilogue

The dream of our present great leaders' predictions like that of our President Abdul Kalam's vision for 2020, will enable Bharat to stand rubbing shoulders with the so-called advanced nations. Linking the knowledge of the universities with the knowledge of Government, Industries and NGOs, will make the dreams of our dedicated freedom fighters will come true. Let us make our flag fly proudly aloft in the comity of nations.

6

Establishing Future Linkages between Universities and NGOs

M. Subbarao

A University is an academic body created to impart education through various educational institutions as per the rules and regulations fixed by the UGC. Every year Universities send lot of human power in to the Society. However, how many could use the knowledge they acquired in these temples. How relevant is the information or content to the contemporary society? How many students are going out with a motivation to change the society or to contribute for the well being of the fellow human beings or to make a difference in a selected sector, with which they are fascinated?

When we were students, intellectuals were blaming Lord Maculae for introducing an education system fit for creating clerks. Everyone was advocating Technical Education. All of us were educated in the Govt. schools and colleges. We almost don't know a private school or college in those days. The entry of private institutions has given a big fillip to the technical education. We have reached a stage where we couldn't have even one student in some of the engineering colleges, in spite of making so many amendments; to admit the least qualified student. Two questions arise here. Are we were talking this type of technical education? And can we run a society with doctors and engineers only?

Every parent want his siblings to become one of the above, why the society doesn't need people with other creative skills which would make lot of difference in people's lives? But as educators or academicians you are helpless, because you are not operating in vacuum and you have to fulfill the demands dictated by the society. With all your commitment and conviction, you can operate within the given periphery for the maximum impact. But how many academicians are committed? Whether the Universities have congenial atmosphere to encourage genuine work'? But does it mean that every academician is involved in the university politics, and all the people in the education are for nothing or all the Universities are useless? No! In spite of all the problems students are coming out and some of them are performing excellent roles in the society. Our aim should be increasing the percentage of this kind of students. All the people in the society should understand, think and work hand in hand for this type of impact in the education system.

I'm an insider to the NGO sector. Every time I meet a Govt. servant, an academician, a politician, a businessman, an industrialist, I use to get hurt about their negative opinion regarding the NGOs. But, this doesn't mean that all the NGOs are angels. We are part of the society. All the good and bad elements would be visible among our organizations also. There are some excellent workers and some typical social contractors among us. Yes! By contractor, what I mean is, a contractor don't know how to make a plan, he would pay money and get it done. Secondly, for getting a contract, he would never hesitate to provide any thing like wine, women or money. By spending all, he would do only a shabby job, which doesn't be any use to the society. Some of the NGOs don't know what is to be written in a proposal, but they could get large projects by following the footsteps of the contractors. But no one has the power to stop them. As long as they are getting money they would be surviving. Whom to blame? Corrupt funding agency representatives, Govt. officials sanctioning projects against percentages? There are NGO politics, funding politics. Unless we understand the sector properly, by not having pragmatic opinion on the NGOs, we couldn't motivate our students in the Universities to work with or to cooperate with the NGOs.

1. Our basic responsibility would be to evolve some basic guidelines, for choosing a good NGO to collaborate with the NGO sector to be given choice to select a good educational institute to work with.
2. Providing an atmosphere of continuous dialogue between the NGO functionaries and interested students. May be all the students are not interested but at least the students in the NSS may be interested.
3. Sharing with all the students in the big gathering once or twice in a year may be very useful to inspire students to involve in the community work.
4. Many of you think an ideal social worker as a fellow wearing handmade khadi, with a beard and shoulder bag. Time has changed, we have transformed a lot. We are no more shouting slogans only. We gave Deendayal bio gas plant, low cost latrine, Micro finance and watershed management to the society. NGOs are running banks organizing trade unions. The NGO sector gave one Rajendra Singh, a Medha Patkar, a Vandana Shiva. a Suneeta Narayan. We have a Vijay Mahajan, a Udaya Kumar. Hundreds, thousands or lakhs of people working without any recognition, toiling for 18 to 20 hours a day, away from their family members for years together.
5. These are scientists, researchers, Engineers, Doctors, lawyers from universities like you. You must be knowing that today you get milk 24 hours because of the intervention or a visionary called Dr. Kurien. The egg production and distribution, regulation is being done by NECC created by one great Dr.Venkateswar Rao.
6. Some groups do not do social work by getting foreign funds. All the interventions among the community, which makes a difference in people's lives, to be considered as social work. Hence we have to include CBOs also in the list of NGOs where our students could learn and serve.

7. Once you define the institutions, the roles and responsibilities would be clear and linkages could be established on a mutually profitable basis. The NGO sector became very diversified today. We need various professionals from different backgrounds. But the question is how do we motivate the youth to work with NGOs.

8. If there is a representation of NGOs, Corporate/ Industrialists and Academicians may be we can sit as three different groups and come out with our expectations, this exercise will make our task easier for the present seminar-cum-workshop.

9. Basically it's the aptitude that is necessary to work in the NGOs rather than the skill itself, secondly capability of applying the wisdom to the practical world to make a difference in the society.

10. Can the universities are capable of inculcating these qualities, if the answer is 'yes' to what extent. If answer is 'no' then what kind of changes you have to make in the curriculum along with teaching and learning methods.

7

University-NGO Linkage

A New Dimension to Extension Programmes

Dr. V. Reghu

Teaching, Research and Extension are the three major roles to be played by the Universities and Institutions of Higher Learning in India. In 1977 the UGC incorporated "Extension" into its policy statement for Higher Education—*"If the University system has to discharge adequately its responsibilities to the entire education system and to the society as a whole it must assure extension as the third important responsibility and give it the same status as teaching and research. This is a new and extremely significant area which should be developed on the basis of high priority."*

The Universities and Colleges with institutional resource and manpower have a social responsibility, to share their knowledge, skills and manpower for the community. It will help the higher education system to gain insights from the socio-cultural realities. The "University-Community interaction" will strengthen the process of learning for students as well as teachers. In brief, this educational process will definitely equip both the community and higher education system to solve the problems of the community. Thus the higher education system will have to prove their social relevance.

According to UGC guidelines the following areas/goals are in focus:

- Continuing Education Programmes at grassroot level and through NIOS/Open Schooling.

- Community harmony and peace education
- Human rights and rights of vulnerable groups
- Environmental issues
- Panchayath and development issues
- Health education for the community
- Women's empowerment
- Social issues and gender issues

To achieve the above goals a well-planned and meaningful "community interaction" is needed. Universities will have to establish a relationship with Governmental Organization, NGOs, Civil Societies, Professional Bodies, Industries, other financial institutions/co-operatives and PRIs. There are number of non-governmental organizations/civil societies in community with strong roots in the community. Majority of them have developed their own infrastructure and community development programmes. The Universities will have to identify such reliable organization with a commendable track record. The Universities with their strong academic and technical resources, can learn further and strengthen their skills through NGO/Community interaction. It is a question of mutual learning for Universities and NGOs, from experience with community programmes and intellectual interaction.

The following are the major roles expected to be played by the Universities:

- Support to NGOs with knowledge resource/ manpower/skills in administration, developing programmes, organization of training programmes, HRD, monitoring evaluation and related areas.
- Conduct of specific courses/need-based programmes to strengthen the Human Resources of NGOs.
- Consultation and technical support in developing innovative programmes aiming at community development.
- Assessment of community needs for planning community development programmes.

- Expertise/knowledge/skill are to be mobilized to improve the quality of programmes.
- Special attention on Human Resource Development and Human Resource Management.
- Focus on research and development based on the specific needs in order to strengthen the quality.
- Improve the quality of programme planning, implementation strategies, monitoring, evaluation and remedial action.
- Working as clearing house, support in documentation.

Extension programme is the major area where linkages can be established with the NGOs and Universities.

University-NGO Linkages—Certain Facilitating Factors

- Mutual understanding, respect and acceptance
- Positive attitude of University Authorities, Teachers, Students and NGO functionaries
- Faith in the programme
- Willingness to learn and act
- Fruitful time management
- Proper support and encouragement from the concerned.
- Mutual learning
- Team work to achieve the goal
- Sense of social commitment
- A climate of tolerance

Some examples cited :

Area	What to do	Who will initiate
1	2	3
1. HRD	Develop courses, training programmes etc.	University/Govt. Agencies
2. HRM	Identify areas/problems/issues etc. and organise management development programmes.	University/NGOs
3. Education	Develop committee system in collaboration with NGOs/peoples participation to strengthen school education/NFE/AE/CE etc. Organise supporting programmes.	NGOs, GOs, Colleges of Education, Department of Education
4. Programmes on HIV/AIDS	Organise awareness programmes for the community with the support of University/College—Teachers, Students and Functionaries, Media Support	University, NGOs, Medical/Nursing Colleges, Teachers and Students
5. Women Empowerment	Awareness programmes, socio-economic programmes by mobilising resources from community/PRI/financial institutions/GOs/Media support etc.	College, University Teachers, PRIs
6. Human Rights Protection	Seminars, workshops, legal support, preparation of relevant materials, media support etc.	Colleges and Students of Law, PRI, ACE & E

(Contd...)

1	2	3
7. Rural Health/ Hygiene	Field visit, study and support. Media support.	Colleges of Nursing, Medical Colleges, Students, NGOs, PRIs
8. Economic Development Programmes	Programmes for socio-economic development, economic empowerment, entrepreneurship development programmes (poverty reduction)	University/Colleges, NGOs with support from financial institutions
9. Training/Research	Training programmes, research projects, HRD programmes	University Department/Colleges/NGOs/GOs
10. Monitoring and Evaluation of Programmes	Monitoring reviews, support for evaluation	Universities, NGOs (A trained team)

University-NGO Linkages—A SWOT Analysis

Strength

- Support mutual learning
- Develop insights
- Leads to innovation
- Strengthen team work
- Involvement of teachers, students and institutions
- Develop social commitment
- Sharing of knowledge and skills
- Practical learning for students
- Enrich experiences

Weakness

- Academic programmes may suffer
- Possibility of misuse of resources
- Time consuming
- Focus on non-academic programmes
- Stereo-typed programmes may dilute the quality

Opportunity

- Students exposure
- Direct learning and understanding
- Insights of teachers and students widen
- More contacts with programmes/people
- Learning from real life
- Development of social commitment
- Development of human resources
- Community development

Threats

- Misuse of the programmes and resources
- Non-cooperation of teachers, students, NGOs, authorities

- Political interference
- Possibility of exploitation
- Problems in continuation of the programmes
- Withdrawal from the programmes (when self-goals are achieved)

In brief: Extension means—the institution (University) *going to community* with its *resources* on recent *advances* in *science and technology* and *improved methods* to change the *outlook of the people* and improve their *quality of life* and *learn from the community*.

8

Changing Role of NGOs in the Development Programmes

Dr. T.G. Ramaiah

As we all are aware, a number of government interventions were made in early 1970s to alleviate rural poverty. In spite of this, a large number of people are still living below poverty line in rural India. The programmes like IRDP could not make much development to eradicate poverty. Some of the evaluation studies on IRDP have highlighted the following deficiencies.

- Lack of technological and institutional capabilities in designing and executing projects utilizing local resources and expertise.
- Beneficiaries with no experience in managing an enterprise.
- Indifferent delivery of credit by banks (high transaction cost, complex procedure, corruption, one-time credit, poor recovery).
- Overcrowding of lending in certain targeting and selection of non-poor.
- Absence of linkage between different components of the IRDP.
- A disturbing feature of the IRDP in several states has been rising indebtedness of the beneficiaries of IRDP.
- Besides, the programme for upgrading skills like TRYSEM, was not dovetailed with IRDP.

However, the programme for women, DWCRA did well in some states (AP, Kerala and Gujarat etc). IRDP and its allied were restructured in 1999 to address some of its shortcomings. The SGSY, which replaced IRDP, is a holistic programme based on a group approach with selection of viable activities.

Similarly, the studies on wage employment programmes (EAS/SGRY) have also identified the following deficiencies.

- Inadequate employment and thin spread of resources; Violation of material-labour (60 : 40) norm.
- Fudging of muster rolls, schemes implemented through contracts universally who sometimes hired outside labourers at lower wages. Unless the deficiencies in wage and self-employment programmes are rectified the rural poverty can not be alleviated. In this connection a number of NGOs played a very important role to implement development programmes for uplift of the poor. The principal objective of the paper has been to analyse the role of NGOs in the Development Programme.

The present study mainly focus on secondary data and a case study of Orugallu Weaker section development, Kothawada village, Warangal district of Andhra Pradesh.

Role of NGO

NGOs as a cohesive alternative force in addressing the needs of the great mass of population in promoting a more responsive and sustained approach to development activities, especially at local level is being increasingly realized both by the national government and the international donors as well. Thus, NGOs are by no means to be looked upon as a new phenomenon and therefore byproduct of the 70s or the 80s. Such organizations in different shapes and sizes and with different names took its origin long before the existence of most of the modern government. Development experience in the third world countries has repeatedly shown the limitations of central government efforts to promote effective rural development at local level. This trend is becoming clear with the world-wide fiscal crisis, the need for increased human resource development within government agencies, and the need to improve the economic livelihood, health, nutritional status and overall well-being of the rural poor. Thus, the rise of the NGOs, both indigenous and foreign, as a strong institutional alternative reflects the growing recognition that the central government and the private sector lack sufficient capacity to respond to the challenge of poverty alleviation. Indeed, the key is to draw on a whole range of institutional and management capabilities at local levels, and to utilize both state and society based channels for development, in order to reduce the burden on the central government and promote effective rural development activities which assist the rural poor.

Characteristics of the Recent NGO Development

(i) The scale and pace with which organizations of such nature have been multiplying and expanding during the last fifteen to twenty years, both in numbers and membership, have no match in past decades of development. A large number of NGOs have come to surface in both developed and developing countries in virtually all areas of public endeavor and are active on either local or national interests.

(ii) Old existing NGOs have started functions on a new area of development not only by orienting and producing support activities to their traditional plan of action for relief and welfare such as agricultural development work by charity organization, religious groups militating for secular causes: new environmental concerns; etc. but also by asserting themselves powerfully much beyond their area of traditional specialization, including domains conventionally regarded as the exclusive prerogative of the government; and

(iii) NGOs, in particular the poor people's organizations, have become internally more sophisticated and better organized, more aware of their power, and thus have increased their militancy and mobilization

capabilities. This strengthening of their internal organization has been complemented by a trend towards establishing linkage systems among NGOs.

Advantages

(i) As these organizations are small and informal, they can respond quickly and directly to development or humanitarian needs and opportunities.

(ii) NGOs can provide grassroot services and dynamism in poor communities in remote areas where the government and other development organization find it difficult to reach.

(iii) The basic responsiveness of NGOs are associated with social, cultural and other aspects of development which are generally ignored by the technical development specialists.

(iv) NGOs already have considerable experience in supporting the strategies, programmes and projects for both the rural and urban majority of poor.

(v) NGOs can help not only in identifying the community needs but also in mobilizing broad and active participation and support for local development activities.

(vi) NGOs have willingness to innovate new development approach techniques, and experiments which may eventually prove quite significant in the context of a broader development activities.

(vii) The operational activities of NGOs are fundamentally related to low overhead cost on salaries, volunteers and appropriate technologies which make the formulated programmes of NGOs at low cost than the official programmes because they are committed to sustainable development approached and to make more use of local resources.

Disadvantages

(i) Due to diverse variety of NGOs and their small scale and disparate aims and operational activities, many NGOs find it difficult to collaborate with other developmental organizations.

(ii) The informal and voluntary nature and scarce resources generally create the problem of weak management of these organizations which can lead to a lack of control over operations and limited accountability for funds.

(iii) It is generally observed that activities of NGO are often individual efforts, implemented without a broader strategy, long term focus, or relationship to work with other institutions.

(iv) Some NGOs operate on the basis of political or religious objectives which can considerably hamper their work with government and other development organizations.

(v) A few NGOs may drift away from innovation, flexibility, independence, and voluntary and participative spirit which actually made them successful in the first place owing to inappropriate support from governmental and multilateral agencies.

Case Study

Recently CAPART has assigned the author a responsibility to evaluate the functioning of "Orugallu weaker section development", Kothawada, Warangal district of Andhra Pradesh. The president of the organisation Smt. P. Amruthamma submitted proposal for financial assistance from CAPART i.e Rs 3,84,300 but CAPART has sanctioned Rs 3,54,300 and advised the organisation to mobilize the remaining Rs 30,000 from beneficiary contribution.

Aims and Objective of the project:

1. Maintain unity among the members of the Sangam

2. Maintain national nntegration
3. Develop uneducated women
4. Teach proper knowledge for poor and uneducated women
5. Offer adult education
6. To provide employment to below poverty line people and increase their income in Handloom and Handicrafts.
7. The project and programmes were aimed at building the capacity of very poor people, children, women and weaker sections so that they could participate effectively in development programmes.

The organisation's main areas are 1. Health and Education 2. Skill upgradation to weaker sections, 3. Economic upliftment of children, women and youth, 4. Welfare of women and children, 5. Awareness campaigns.

The president and all members of the Sangam belonged to weaver community who were engaged in weaving saris and other items like bed sheets, swings, wall hangings, carpets, file covers, different designs of hand bags, dress materials for ladies. These products were sold at Kothapeta, Warangal district and Hyderabad. The NGO not only taught them technical skills but also helped them in marketing their products. Through this intervention the beneficiaries acquired entrepreneurial skills, market exposure, and above all, self-confidence in building viable, sustainable self employment opportunities to participate in market economy.

Conclusion

From the above discussion, it is clear that Govt. Institutions/Department alone can not deliver the needed efforts in the development programme launched immediately after independence. The Non-Government Organizations initially played the role of educationists creating awareness on development programmes launched by the Government from time to time in the primary, secondary and territory sectors.

Appreciating the service-motto efforts of the Non-Government Offices, the Govt. itself assigned the NGOs the role of awareness building through mass campaigning development programmes and also more particular in rural development programmes. Among rural development programmes area development programmes such as DPAP, DDP, IWDP programmes where watershed development was taken up on approach for area development conserving soil and water involving the local communities. In such participatory programmes, NGOs through their inherent ingenuity adopted techniques which resulted in successful community mobilization for effective participation. The Self Help Groups, watershed users associations, technical teams are some of the bodies promoted by NGOs in implementation of the rural development programmes launched by Government of India from time to time.

Of late, in addition to capacity building, community mobilization and awareness building NGOs are playing the role of facilitators in the participatory rural development programmes. Many of the banking institutions are highly dependent on the federations of SHGs who in many cases are the successful NGOs playing the key role in effective repayment of the loan as well as the successful implementation of the programme. Thus, in many parts of the country even coordination of various institutions collective purchase of inputs/ raw material and bulk sale of produce of this federation is facilitated by NGOs.

Thus the NGOs plays a pivotal role in all the development programmes through multifarious roles ranging from awareness building, community mobilization, capacity building, coordination, collective bargaining and facilitation of community involvement in management of ongoing rural development programmes.

9

University and NGOs' Partnership

B.S. Vasudeva Rao

Resources have been defined as "Comprising those basic services without which primary, secondary and territory productive activities cannot function". Also referred to encourage investment later in other directly productive activities. Simply stating, resources includes development services such as research, evaluation, monitoring and training. Both the universities and Non-Governmental Agencies on their own have been found wanting an efficient provider of infrastructure. The solution to the complex problem of financing infrastructure could probably lie in a symbiotic relationship or university non-governmental organization partnership between the two sectors based on their inherent strengths and weaknesses. The universities and NGOs sectors usually have distinctive but potentially complementary role to play. Such partnerships have the potential to enable the delivery of high quality of infrastructure services.

Universities are very important institutions in any Nation. Pandit Jawaharlal Nehru, the first Prime Minister of independent India, once said that "A university stands for humanism, for tolerance, for truth. It stands for the onward march of the human race towards even higher objectives. If our universities discharge their duties adequately, it is well with the Nation and people". Universities are important means for exploring, generating, conserving and transmitting knowledge. At present junction universities have to play critical role in serving the human society. They have to provide for leadership in voluntary sector, political, administration, industry and ecological preservation. They also must enable the Nation free from want, disease, ignorance and illiteracy by the application of student power, humanistic, scientific and technical knowledge to real world problems. (Schulze William J). Volunteerism basically refers to the spirit of action carried on by an individual on his/her own will for welfare and development of the people and society. In recent years there is a growth in terms of reorganization of volunteerism. This is due to factors like growing social consciousness and sense of social responsibilities among people especially the students and youth. The enrolment of 17.50 lakh students in National Service Scheme, growing establishment of youth clubs, joining in NCC (12 lakh approximately) and Bharat Scouts and Guides are examples for student interest in voluntary action. Some of the functions and characteristics of NGOs and universities are presented to identify similarities and advantage of partnership between the two.

Universities

1. Faculty are enriched with knowledge and acquainted with research and extension activity
2. Vast student power
3. Both teachers and students are respected by the society
4. Flexibility in job situation; they can plan their teaching programme and inculcate innovative thinking in teaching-learning-research activity
5. Macro-level approach in general and micro-level approach in class situation
6. Adequate library and computer facility
7. There is no elements of bureaucratic behaviour among teachers and students
8. The university faculty indirectly is nearer to society through parents

9. Infrastructural facilities are more
10. It is a self-governing and autonomous community enjoying 'freedom'

Non-Governmental Organisations

1. Limited manpower but with voluntary nature
2. Trained only in specific area
3. Respected by the people in their field areas
4. The programmes started with specific planning and objectives, but this can be changed according to geographical area, stakeholders, sometimes depending on nature of funding agency.
5. Micro-level approach in implementing the programme.
6. Inadequacy of infrastructural facilities.
7. Limited resources in many cases
8. The NGOs are nearer to society with regard to the effective welfare activity
9. The NGOs acts as a catalyst between government developmental activities and needy people
10. The volunteer worker has more accessibility among people than government officials. Similarly in the case of students and teaching faculty of academic bodies.

What is UNGOP?

The utilization of university faculty and students for the development of society in general and community in particular is the philosophy of UNGOP. The students are involved in constructive work under the supervision of faculty and during holidays and as a part of curriculum. In this regard, I noted once upon a time the Madras Government initiated a project that the youth who worked in rural areas at least two years will be given preference in employment. A UNGOP is essentially a collaboration between the university and the Non-Government sector to create a structure in which improved Value-for-Service can be achieved through the involvement of NGO sector due to enhanced scope for innovation and allocation of risk to the party best able to manage it without undermining the universities overall responsibility to the students for the quality of the services provided. It aims to create a "win-win-situation" for the university, the NGO and the users—the university wins as it is able to fulfill its mandated responsibilities of providing adequate service to its students, the NGO sector wins as it gets a responsible rate of return on its investment while the users benefit from the availability, affordability and accessibility of quality infrastructure services.

A large number of infrastructural projects languish through years of sub-optimal implementation due to lack of funds and committed manpower. This leads to enormous cost overruns and escalation, growing overheads and inflation. It is essential to remember that the opportunity cost of this situation is prohibitive leading to regressive pricing in many cases where the poor and up paying more than the rich. The fundamental principles of UNGOP are that the University and NGO sector are responsible for the research, development, evaluation, monitoring and community service. This basic scheme has numerous variations depending on the risk allocation between the university and NGO sector. The utilization of student service for the development of community through NGOs is the philosophy of UNGOP. The basic idea is to provide the services by the students not only at the least cost but also to ensure the quality and timeliness of services delivered. This comprises of monetary comparison wherein the cost of the preferred UNGOP project is compared with the cost of traditional public sector, expressed in terms of discounted cashflows over the life of the UNGOP understanding and the non-monetary comparison which takes into account many factors, which are difficult to quality but at the same time contribute significantly to value for service since they are of crucial importance to the university and the wider public/students. Examples include speed on project delivery, quality of service and students exposure. Standardization of understanding basically aims to provide some sort of benchmark for future UNGOP transactions on the basis of past experience. Partnerships are standardized keeping in mind the uses relevant to different sectors such as sharing of risks, financing and pricing issues. This helps in reducing the time and cost of negotiation by enabling all parties concerned to agree on a range of areas that can follow a standard approach without extended negotiations. While there are a number of students indicating what approach suits which sector, the one common factor identified by these studies is that UNGOP approach succeeds better where performance parameters are relatively simple and are amenable to a high degree of standardization. However, it should be kept in mind that there are clear limitations to standardization as different projects have their specific difference and risk. To optimize on project preparation costs and to lend credibility to the selection process of the project, the implementing agency would prepare the detailed project report, which would inter alia set out the detailed standards and specification for programme. The process of selection of a NGO could be through an open competitive monitoring process to select someone who has the necessary technical skills and financial resources to implement the project as well as one who could offer the best value for service to the users. But more often than not, the NGOs with the least cost are awarded the project. This ensures objectivity and transparency of the monitoring process since a financial parameter is easily quantifiable.

Benefits

- Keeping in mind fiscal constraints and massive investment needs in infrastructure, NGO sector participation helps in leveraging scare budgetary resources.
- The university retains the ownership of the asset created.
- The NGO sector not only provides finance but also innovative and modern managerial, administrative and technical support.
- Transfer of construction risk, operation risk, revenue risk and financing risk to the concessionaire.

- Subsidies are made more efficient (better targeted and transparent).
- The past experiences suggest that both time and cost overruns are minimized with the involvement of the university and NGO sector.
- Participation by university to provide policy level and statutory support.
- Involvement of universities helps in expedating and resolving major bottlenecks:
    1. Increase in manpower with less expenditure
    2. Availability of youth and trained persons
    3. Constant monitoring of the ongoing activity
    4. Useful evaluation outcomes.
    5. Cost effective and voluntary base.
- University may consider "viability gap funding" for making ongoing projects involving NGO viable.
- Commitment and participation by university to enhance stakeholders' confidence enabling mobilization of cheaper funds.

Both the universities and NGOs have similar characteristics like flexibility in decision-making, better communication agents and effective coordination.

Significant Role of Students

The student volunteers of National Service Scheme (NSS) in junior colleges, degree colleges and universities have played a significant role in community development. The volunteers numbering approximately 17.50 lakh doing good service particularly in the areas such as education, health, hygiene and their involvement to create awareness about HIV/AIDS among masses. Through their regular activities such as rural camps, they contributed to establish community infrastructures whose value may be crores of rupees, for example laying roads, cleaning of drainages and rebuilt of river sides and so on. When compared to government activity it is with limited expenditure without the presence of middle man.

Raj Kishore Mishra highlighted three contributions made by NSS volunteers in a paper projects undertaken by the NSS volunteers in Madhya Pradesh which were technically assessed and evaluated by the Rural Engineering Department of the State. The total value of these projects was Rs. 6.28 lakh. If only a fraction of such projects undertaken by the NSS volunteers throughout the country could be assessed and evaluated, it would undoubtedly run into crores of rupees. Take the case of Chandigarh's famous Sukhna lake. Its desiltation owes a lot to the voluntary efforts put in by the NSS volunteers of the Union Territory. In yet another path-breaking venture, the NSS volunteers of Bangalore University have joined hands with the Indian Institute of Science, the Ministry of Environment and Forest Government of the India and the State Department of Environment and Forest in developing a 400 acre bio-diversity park in Bangalore. This effort has own allround encomiums for the NSS volunteers, including a pat from the State Chief Minister. Further, in literacy campaigns Mass Programmes of Functional Literacy and other programme were designed to involve student to eradicate illiteracy. Under this programme each student was entrusted to undertake "each one teach one" or "each one teach five" and obtained successful result. The interaction between university faculty, students and NGOs in societal development will give good notable result in upliftment of peoples' life. This partnership benefits both university and NGOs in societal transformation.

The NGOs can utilize the technical expertise of faculty and by involving students, the activity will be speed up, accepted by stakeholders, cost-effective with limited time span. Further, the students will benefit by utilizing their leisure and holidays in constructive work, understanding the nature of stakeholders' living conditions and in some case getting financial assistance for their studies. In present days with the limited association with volunteer sector, some of the drawbacks noticed specifically from small and new NGOs—lack of guidance, inadequate training skills, some problems in preparing budget for financial assistance, in preparing project proposal, unable to pay high salaries for technical persons. These constraints may be overcome by association with institution of high learning. From the student point of view after completion of the studies instead of idle, they can be absorbed in any voluntary sector or they can start their own with this experience The universities and NGOs have similar functions and characteristics like flexibility in decision making, better communication agents to society and effective coordinators. The intellectual efficiency of university and effective work commitment of NGOs put together will yields considerable results in improving the life pattern of poor and ecological development. Hence, the authors suggest the NGOs can associate with academicians and take the help of students and faculty of universities and involve them in their endeavor.

REFERENCES

Pradeep R Mehendiratta (1984) "*University Administration in India and the USA Approaches, Issues and Implications: A Comparative Study*" Oxford & IBH Publishing Co.

Raj Kishore Mishra (2001) "Youth Volunteerism in India," Published in "*Yojana*" Vol. 45, December.

Vasudeva Rao, B.S. (2004) "*Evaluation Studies*" Edited Volume, The Associated Publishers, New Delhi.

10

Collaboration Programmes through Partnership

Dr. Bhalba Vibhute

Partnerships amongst stakeholders has been recognised worldover as the powerful instrument in managing change. The importance and the need of partnerships amongst academic institutions and other sectors of the society has been recognised by the UNESCO. UNESCO sponsored World Conferences on Higher Education held at Paris in 1998 emphasised the need of collaboration in the following words: "Partnerships and alliances amongst stakeholders—national and institutional policymakers, teaching and related staff, researchers and students and administrative and technical personnel in institutions of higher education, the world of work, community groups—is a powerful force in managing change. Also non-governmental are key actors in the process. Henceforth, partnership based on common interest, mutual respect and credibility should be a prime matrix for renewal."

Community Engagement in Indian Higher Education

Education has been recognised as a powerful instrument of social change and hence in a democratic country like India it becomes imperative, particularly on the part of educational institutions that educational needs of the community should be taken care of the formal education system, though systematically formed and implemented seriously, by itself, due to its own limitations, is unable to cater to the changing educational needs of the whole community. Hence the ways and means by which educational needs of the community can be met were thought of and non-formal system approach has been adopted in Indian higher education and extension got prominence. "It was way back in 1964-66 that the Kothari Commission first articulated the concept of Extension and the TRINITY of Teaching, Research and Extension. A Commission even stated that Extension was essential for:

- making education relevant to real life situations.
- for preventing the alienation of the education from society.
- for developing in the education a sense of responsibility towards society.
- for deepening the teacher's knowledge through a wider exposure to the real life situations (UGC Guidelines, 2004).

In 1977 the UGC first incorporated Extension into its Policy Statement for Higher Education as: "If University system has to discharge adequately its responsibilities to the entire education system, and to the society as a whole, it must assume extension as the third important responsibility and give it the same status as teaching and research (UGC Guidelines, 2004). In 1980s the process of establishing Departments in Indian Universities to look after the functions of extension education took momentum and under the leadership of the University Grants Commission Department of Adult and Continuing Education and Extension Work were established in Indian Universities. The community engagement activities, such as eradication of illiteracy, continuing of population education, legal literacy, planning forum were entrusted to these departments. Since then the focus of the activities has remained the same with some modifications. But the Xth Plan Guideline of the UGC on Adult and Continuing Education has emphasised the need of starting of academic courses, Associate Degree/ Diploma Courses as continuing education, Leardship/HRD. Quality of Life Improvement Programmes (QLIP), Individual Interest Promotion Programmes (IIPP), Social and Citizenship

Role Programmes, Equivalency Programmes (EPs), becoming resource centre etc. Xth Plan Guidelines also encouraged to start E-learning centres to offer online courses and also to establish students counselling centres. As on today 73 such departments are working in Indian Universities.

Since the inception of departments of Adult and Continuing Education, they have adopted a collaboration and networking approach for implementing its programmes. In making efforts to take education to the people beyond reach it has become imperative on our part to have collaboration with the different institutions from society, major partners would remain to be the affiliated colleges in the words of Rekha S. Sen, "Collaboration and networking to provide education is going to become imperative and we want to cut costs in education, enhance the outreach/jurisdiction of the institution and make available a variety of courses without constraints of time and space". The need of the collaboration and networking has been emphasised in the Xth Plan Guidelines (p.-7) as: "Programme to support and evaluate TLC, PLC, CE, Sarva Shikshan Abhiyan, Women's Empowerment etc. in collaboration with or for the NLM, State Literacy Mission (SLM), Centers for Women's Studies, Population Education Centres, Open Universities, People's Organisations, Community Based Organisations, Civil Societies and others.

Shivaji University Perspective

Shivaji University, Kolhapur (Maharashtra/India), established in 1962 at Kolhapur, opted motto of taking University to the masses and accordingly tries to cater the educational needs of the people from the four districts (now three districts) by organising educational programmes both in formal and non-formal education. The DACEE established in 1984 in this University has been engaged in taking education to unreached by launching different type of activities which include eradication of illiteracy, continuing and population education, legal literacy, planning forum, field outreach, training/orientations/conferences for students, teachers, NGOs, etc. (this includes in service training's), diplomas, resource centre etc. For implementation of such programmes the DACEE, from its inception, has adopted collaboration with networked approach.

The Partnerships

DACEE in order to facilitate needbased educational programmes formed partnerships with affiliated colleges, University departments, other Universities, Governmental Agency and also with Non-Government Organisations. Michael Neil defines collaboration as "an active working partnership supported by some kind of institutional commitment". Such inter-institutional collaboration help fulfill the needs of the concerned institutions and their clients.

Why Collaboration?

Inter-Institutional Collaboration helps to achieve the following:

1. It promotes inter-institutional cooperation.
2. Minimisation of cost by which maximum people can be benefited
3. Sharing of resources at the disposal of institutions, such as human resources and their skills, information resources, laboratories, accommodation, libraries, managerial resources, financial resources etc.
4. Reaching to the unreached at remotest places and taking education to their doorsteps
5. Opening doors to adults learners for life-long learning programmes.
6. Making available variety of need-based programmes without any constraints.
7. Widens organisational base and helps promoting sense of extended family and develops group dynamics.
8. Solves problems such as recognition, quality control, accreditation certification etc.

9. Maximum use of scarce resources.
10. Help establish relationship between "World of Knowledge" and "World of Work."

Collaborative Programme

Warna Experience

Among the various activities that the DACEE of Shivaji University has been undertaking is the activity of institution-based continuing education courses. The department develops curricula based on the needs of target groups with the help of experts. The focus of such courses is to provide opportunity to college students, out-of-school youth, unemployed youth, women, promotion seekers, persons requiring upgrading skills in personality development and also opening up income generation channels. It is advised by the UGC that Vocational Career Oriented "courses and programmes for people at different socio-economic and educational levels for the acquisition of marketable vocational skills according to the needs and demands of urban and rural, local, national and international markets" be conducted by DACEE's.

DACEE of Shivaji University right from its inception has adopted this approach for implementing its programmes. As said elsewhere in this paper we have established linkages with different types of institutions and Warna Bazar is one of such institution where we run one month duration course on "Salesmanship". Warnanagar is known for network of cooperative institutions all over the country. Warnanagar, 25 km away from Kolhapur is the pioneering institute in cooperative sector. Late Tatyasaheb Kore, a visionary, started cooperative movement in Warna area by establishing Warna Cooperative Sugar Factory and that was followed by establishing other cooperative units in that region. Warna dairy milk products are well known in the country and abroad. Another unit run by Warna region Cooperative Consumer Mandal, Warnanagar is the WARNA BAZAR with which we have collaboration. Warna Bazar is one of the leading consumer societies in rural India. It has got privilege of becoming first consumer cooperative stores in India to achieve turnover of more than 51 crore rupees (2003-2004). It is a unique cooperative unit as far as the membership distribution on genderwise basis is concerned. Out of 9808 members 7581 are female and only 2227 are male. In other words, 77 percentage of member population belongs to the female category. It has two department stores located in Warnanagar and Wadgaon and 36 retail outlets in its service area. 461 staff working in these centers have their contribution to the growth of Warna Bazar

Salesmanship Course

From the last ten years we have been conducting one month duration course on Salesmanship in Warnabazar at Warnanagar with a view to:

- Provide hands on training to youth in salesmanship.
- Provide in-service training to persons working in Consumer Stores.
- Opening up employment opportunities in marketing.

Course Details

– **Medium of instruction**	:	Marathi
– **Duration**	:	One month
– **Course objectives**	:	To make participants aware of the techniques of good salsemanship. To Provide them an opportunity to carry the activities of salesmanship.
– **Course Description**	:	1. Cooperation principles and nature, cooperative organisations, education and training in cooperation, review of cooperative Movement in India. 2. Consumers movement in India—a historical perspective, Departmental stores, super bazars. 3. Methods of purchase, account keeping, management, control and reporting in consumer cooperatives. 4. Sales management—objectives and importance, sales policies—need and importance, types of salesmans, salesman training, ideal salesman.

5. Types and salient features of consumer, consumer psychology, rights and duties of consumer, consumer movement, consumer salesman relationship.
6. Time management in consumer cooperative management and its importance.
7. Marketing management in consumer cooperative management and its importance.
8. Plan and layout in consumer cooperative management and its importance.
9. Stores operation in consumer cooperative management and its importance.
10. Mission of consumer cooperative management.

- **Pre-Requisites** : S.S.C.
- **Delivery Methods** : Lecture, demonstration and practicles.
- **Course Components** : Text, practicle, demos (print, video films, films etc.)

Ten Year Partnership

The tables 10.1 and 10.2 show the status of partnership in enrollment trend and employability strength of the course.

It can observed that:

1. In Warna Bazar alone 89 participants from Salesmanship Course got employment.
2. In other Bazar at Phaltan, Satara, Mumbai, Raigad, Alibag, Gadhinglaj, Karad, Kankawali, Kalamba, Thane, Kirloskarwadi, Sangli, Mangaon, Majalgao, Latur, Devarashtre, Akluj, Tumbharni, Yedenipani, Islampur, Aurangabad, Solapur, Chalisgao 82 participants got employment.
3. It is also observed that more than 50 per cent of the remaining candidates have started their own shops at their locality.

How it happened?

1. Mutual understanding of collaborative partners.
2. Well spelled out objectives and goals of partnership.
3. Flexible approach which helped to accommodate innovations and also to revision of the terms and conditions.
4. Clear understanding as far as the work role and responsibilities are concerned.
5. Common interest of both the partners.
6. Credibility of both the institutions in the minds of the people.

Partnership between DACEE and Warna Bazar has proved the need of collaboration programmes through partnership.

Table 10.1: Enrolment and Achievement of the Salesmanship Course during 1996-2005

Year	Enrolment	Achievement
1996	35	33
1997	32	31
1998	31	31
1999	41	39
2000	48	44
2001	50	47
2002	43	37
2003	47	46
2004	45	43
2005	51	51
Total	**423**	**402**

Note: It can be observed from the table that percentage of candidates successfully completing the course is above 94 per cent.

Table 10.2: Employment Generation through Salesmanship Course during 1996-2005

Year	Employed in Warna Bazar	Employed in Other Bazars	Total
1996	8	6	14
1997	8	4	12
1998	5	6	11
1999	13	6	19
2000	10	6	16
2001	11	6	17
2002	7	13	20
2003	7	10	17
2004	6	13	19
2005	14	12	26
Total	**89**	**82**	**171**

Conclusion

In the words of Prof. K. B. Pawar (2002)—"collaboration between different institutions is facilitated if they have common goals and objectives. It is especially useful when the strengths of collaborating institutions complement each other. This leads to showing of both work and responsibilities. Hence while working for partners, apart from mutual interest, a complementarily in strength has to be examined. The complementarities...may be on macro or micro-scale. Thus universities, that provide the strong academic background required for a project, need to collaborate with industrial units, that possess practical know-how on production process". To sum up, collaboration programmes in higher education encourage community education. It helps to understand the skills needed for communication and efficient functioning of the institutions and also generates employment at the local level. This is possible if we choose right partners who are well motivated and have clear goals of community development.

REFERENCES

1. Networking of Universities, Research Institutions and Industry, ALU, New Delhi, 2002.

2. Tenth Plan UGC Scheme on Adult and Continuing Education, Extension & Field Outreach, UGC, New Delhi, 2004.

3. Proceedings of International Conferences on "Collaborative Networked Learning 14 November, 1998.

4. Annual Report of Warna Bazar 2003-04.

5. Documents of the Salesmanship Course, DACEE, Shivaji University, Kolhapur 1996-2005.

11

Linkage between the University and the Corporate NGO

Renuka Narang

The Departments of Adult and Continuing Education and Extension (DACEE) have the mandate in the Tenth Plan Guidelines to conduct a wide range of programs such as:

1. Courses in Andragogy
2. Vocational and Career-oriented programs
3. Offering an Associate Degree in Continuing Education
4. Leadership and Human Resource Development Programs
5. Life Improvement Programs
6. Individual Interest programs
7. Social and Citizenship Role Awareness Programs
8. Conduct of Programs with the support of resources from the government, NGOs and others
9. Equivalency Programs and

   the establishment of an award of an academic credit to students who participate in such programs.

In carrying out the above programs and activities the DACEE take the assistance of NGOs and government agencies. The support from NGOs could be for training and research, for funds, for expertise, etc. In a similar manner the DACEE extend support to the NGOs for the conduct of their programs and activities. While the DACEE has developed linkages with voluntary agencies, as of today the DACEE have not actively engaged themselves with the NGOs set up by the Corporate houses.

The UGC Guidelines recommend that the DACEE develop linkages with industry and business for the development and conduct of a range of programs. Efforts of the DACEEs have generally been limited to obtaining sponsorships, carrying out student placement exercises, carrying out collaborative programs, etc., e.g. in the University of Mumbai the DACEE introduced the Industry Orientation Project for students and undertook a collaborative exercise for computer education with Tata Infotech Ltd. It also took the help of industry for the introduction of e-Learning in the university.

Each Corporate House has set up a Voluntary Agency or a Foundation. Some of the well known Corporate NGOs are the Tata Trusts, Azim Premji. Foundation, Nanhi Kali Project of the Mahindra Trust, Mahindra Foudation, the Computer Based Functional Literacy Project of Tata Consultancy Services, the Aditya Birla Center for Community Initiatives and Rural Development, etc. Recently the Tata Trusts were given an award by the Economics Times.

The Tata Trusts carry out a range of charitable activities which involve mainly the sanction of grants for scholarships, healthcare, awards, etc. The Azim Premji Foudation aims at making a tangible impact on identified social issues by working in active partnership with the government and others. In particular the Foundation is dedicated to the Universalization of Elementary Education in India. It has developed a Learning Guarantee Program and a Computer Aided Learning Program and introduced these in the states of Rajasthan, Tamil Nadu, Karnataka, etc. It has developed CDs in Tamil and other languages for use by the children at the primary school level.

The Computer Based Functional Literacy Program (CBFL) of Tata Consultancy Services involves the conduct of literacy programs for the achievement of "reading literacy" in 30 to 40 hours using a software of literacy lessons developed by its employees in several languages such as Telegu, Tamil, Hindi, Marathi, and Bengali. It has recently developed literacy lessons in Urdu which it wants to field test. It aims at accelerating the rate of reading literacy achievement in the country through the use of software developed by it. For achieving this goal it requires the achievements of the CBFL program to be authenticated through research so that it has a strong base for proposing that the government of India take it up as a national strategy for enhancing the achievement of the rate of reading literacy.

The Naanhi Kali Project of K. C. Mahindra Trust is an ambitious project aimed at helping the underprivileged girl child in India. The project's principal goal is to promote primary education for the underprivileged girl child in both the urban and rural areas. It encourages people to adopt a girl child and sponsor her education. At present it is looking after 1,700 girl children with the help of 18 NGOs. The Mahindra Foundation on the other hand contributes support during natural calamities such as drought, floods, earthquakes, etc.

The Aditya Birla Center for Community Initiatives and Rural Development headed by Smt. Rajashree Birla has as its vision.

"To actively contribute to the social and economic development of communities in which we operate. In doing so, build a better, sustainable way of life for the weaker sections of society and raise the country's human development index."

Each company of the Aditya Birla Group has set up a Jan Seva Trust (JST) an NGO funded by the company. The aim of the JST is to develop the villages surrounding a plant by focusing on education, healthcare and family welfare, vocational training, provision of safe drinking water, construction of roads, sanitation systems, etc. as well as working on social issues such as widow remarriage, mass marriages, etc. Actually each company adopts a specific number of villages to be developed as "model villages". The Aditya Birla Group has a budget of about Rs 65 to 70 crores for this community based work. It hires social workers to carry out the work of the JST.

The NGOs established by the Corporate Sector offer an opportunity to the DACEE to involve their students in their work. It is suggested that since the DACEE work through their colleges in the community, a Corporate House close to a college could be identified and students could be involved in their work. An academic credit could be awarded for the student's participation in such Extension Work. A student in working with the Corporate NGO would also be exposed to the Corporate culture at the ground level which would be an incentive along with the incentive for an academic credit.

Secondly it is suggested that the DACEE join up their programs with that of the Corporate House so that they can work together with them for the uplift of the masses. Since the Corporate Houses have definite budgets the DACEE by working with them would not have to undertake the task of raising funds.

Further Corporate Houses need manpower to execute their projects. They have always looked to the Schools of Business for students who have specialized in HR or they have recruited personnel from the Schools of Social Work. They have apparently not heard about the DACEE and neither have the DACEE ever trained their students for such a role. It is suggested that the DACEE develop curriculum or suitably modify their course curriculum so that a human resource suitable for employment by the Corporate NGO is prepared. A part of such a curriculum would involve field work through placement with the Corporate House. Further the academic staff of the DACEE could work as consultants for the Corporate House by undertaking research work, say, for example for the CBFL program of TCS or work as trainers or carry out surveys for them, etc.

Thus it is strongly suggested that the DACEE take steps to develop linkages with the NGOs and Foundations established by the Corporate Houses thus expanding their field of operations and their network.

Theme II

Human Resources Availability and Requirements for NGOs: The Role of Universities

12

Convert Human Resource into Resourceful Assets

C. Ramakanta Sharma

Traditionally resources used in any organization are classified into five categories, popularly known as five Ms—money, machine, material, method and man. Of these, man alone has mind. Man can think and decide. Even other resources can be controlled by man. Yet, the importance of other resources was understood much earlier than that of man. The situation is changed due to advent of information technology and globalisation, lifestyles of the people, policies and programmes of the Central and State governments. Success of welfare programmes, policies, projects etc., depends on excellent human resources. Human resource is an important and valuable asset of the organization. A separate ministry has been formed at the Centre as well as in many States to look after the development of human resources. Also, in every industry both public and private sector, separate department of HRD is established to recruit, train, guide the employees and coordinate the work and cooperate in achieving targets. Hence, efforts are on in many organizations to convert their human resources into resourceful assets. Resource asset is one that generates further resources. Both idle resource and idle asset are bad. Efforts must be made to maintain assets in functional, resourceful condition.

The following examples make the idea clear:

Water is a resource. Water collected in a dam is an asset. When the same water is used for irrigation and for generating it becomes a resourceful asset. Metal is a resource. Machines made of the metal become an asset. When that machine manufactures some products it becomes a resourceful asset. Here, three steps are necessary—identifying man suitable for the job —Resource; training him for the job skills—Asset; and giving job opportunities to him for utilizing his skills—Resourceful asset. Mere acquiring educational qualification in social sciences is not enough to work in the Non-Government Organisations (NGOs) The staff recruited should be given suitable orientation training about the nature of work, objectives of the NGOs, targets fixed, organisation's mission. Create awareness among the employees of NGOs about the organization and educate them in functional areas. In addition to the above, the employees should also be given training in the following areas:

1. Qualities of Inner Beauty.
2. Character building.
3. Communication skills and human relations.
4. Social responsibility—Service mind.
5. Time management and discipline
6. Leadership qualities, team building, goal achievement.
7. Employer-Employee relations.
8. Stress management.
9. Ethics and values.
10. Volunteers and public relations.

Skills may be divided into two kinds. One is professional skills and another is management techniques which are to be learned after entering into the NGOs through orientation/training/refresher courses etc. There are number of NGOs functioning to serve the poor people suffering from various socio-economic problems, diseases, physically handicapped etc. These people needs human help in different forms to lead healthy and happy life. NGOs have come forward to shoulder the responsibility of these people with dedication and commitment. In view of the above, it is proposed to have "HRD CENTRE

FOR NGOs" headed by a professionally qualified and experienced Social Scientist or Chief Training Executive with necessary supporting staff who should be able to work with professional and social culture. The following suggestions may be examined, discussed and give final shape, if accepted, for providing budget.

1. The finances may be shared by the NGOs of every district depending on their annual budget.
2. The Central and State governments should also be provide finances to the centre.
3. The funding agencies in India and abroad may be asked to allot a fixed percentage of funds to meet the training needs of the staff both administrative and field staff.
4. The International organizations should earmark the funds required for this purpose while considering the proposals for sanction of the project/scheme.

The above setup will serve as a uniform procedure and training needs for all the NGOs', so that the HRD Centre would finalise the schedule of the training/orientation/refresher programmes periodically once in a year or two depending on the needs and requirements of the NGOs'. This system will pave the way to drive the NGOs with quality of administration, quality of profession and convert the human resources as resourceful assets to serve the poor people with human face and human values as per vision and mission of the NGOs.

13

Collaborative Roles of University and NGO for Life Education and Better Services

M.C. Reddeppa Reddy

Introduction

One of the goals of the University Grants Commission (UGC) is to transform the university system into an active instrument for social change through the institutionalization of extension as the third dimension and by ensuring that the university system is learner friendly and pro-lifelong learning. It is clearly stated in the Xth Plan UGC Scheme on Adult, Continuing Education, Extension and Field Outreach (2004) that through the dimension of teaching, there is dissemination of knowledge, through research new knowledge is generated and through the dimension of extension there is application of knowledge to real life situations and service to the society which further leads to generation of new knowledge and experiences. For many years in India, voluntary organizations alone were in the field of extension and delivery of services to the rural people. Of late, the Government and the Universities have entered the field. With the superior and adequate financial administration and academic ability, these two agencies easily manage to become more important than voluntary agencies. But voluntary agencies have certain merits, which make them equally important. These organizations work with the people and for the people. Government and university units work more for the people, but formalism make the two agencies a less effective so far as the ultimate objective is concerned. Moreover, the knowledge which the students gained from the university is inadequate and not too relevant to secure jobs either in government or non-governmental organizations. Hence, there is a need to collaborate these three main stakeholders of development and social service for enriching the quality of education on one hand and for delivering social service activities to the rural communities with desired level, on the other. An attempt has been made in this paper to review the status and nature of NGOs' role of University in strengthening of NGOs and expanding services of these organizations in improving the quality of College/University education and utilizing the services of students and teachers in developmental and social service activities. The paper also offers certain suggestions for selecting suitable NGOs for better collaboration.

Present Status of NGOs

NGOs have come to occupy an important position in the country. According to one estimate the number of NGOs in the country touches 30 thousands. This growth has not been geographically uniform. More than that, the number of Voluntary Organizations does not correspond to the size of the population in the states. Highly populated states such as Uttar Pradesh and Madhya Pradesh, for instance, have few Voluntary organizations. Maharastra, West Bengal, Gujarat, Andhra Pradesh and Kerala on the other hand have more number of Organizations. Over 30,000 registered associations under the Foreign Contribution Regulatory Act (FCRA) and more then 500 other associations obtain permission every year to receive foreign contributions. The annual receipt in the voluntary sector has swelled to over Rs. 5,000 crores. Their presence is felt among the tribes, women in the organized sector, destitutes, children, the aged, sex workers, handloom weavers, the blind and other similar neglected and marginalized sections of society. NGOs could penetrate these segments of population where assistance was required but hard to come by.

Role of Voluntary Organizations

The voluntary organizations are accessible to people and they are sensitive to the needs of the community. They give personal touch to the services they offer. They are capable of bringing people together and motivate them to participate in the developmental process.

Flexibility in approach helps the NGOs invent appropriate solutions to the problems they confront. They can adjust to the needs of clients. They have been perceived as flexible, participatory, inexpensive and are able to reach the poor better. The programmes they undertake are people-centered and people-oriented. Home Ministry officials point out that nearly 13,800 registered organizations submit their annual accounts to the Ministry but their total number could be around 30,000. Quoting official figures, the representatives of NGOs say that only 6.6 per cent of foreign funds were used for religious purposes. The Northern states only received 2.09 per cent of the total foreign funding whereas the four Southern States—Andhra Pradesh, Tamil Nadu, Karnataka, Kerala—receive 49.55 per cent of the total foreign fundings. The total foreign funding of NGOs in 1999-2000 was Rs. 3,924.63 crores, a 15 per cent increase over the previous year. As long as poverty is endemic in the country, with about 26 per cent of the population below the official poverty line, which is a very large chunk of population. India certainly needs action outside the government boundaries for solving issues of livelihood, empowerment of deprived sections, women, of education, healthcare and so on. The case for social action is indeed compelling from the Universities besides the non-governmental organizations which are employing the graduates and postgraduates in extending the services to the poor.

Pioneers in the Voluntary Sector in India

Different pioneers have contributed to the development of the nation through voluntary efforts. They include: Dayananda Saraswathi, Rajaram Mohan Roy, Keshab Chandra Sena, Iswar Chandra Vidyasagar, Swamy Vivekananda, Loka Manya Tilak, Rabendranath Tagore, Ranade, Kare, Annia

Beasant, Syed Ahmed Khan, The Begums of Bhopal, Kamala Devi Chatopadhyay, Aravind Ghosh, Madan Mohan Malavaya, Gandhiji, Durgabai Deshmukh, etc.

However, there is reluctance, even visible resistance, in certain quarters against acceptance of the value of sharing responsibility for development with non-governmental organizations. However, there is a sweeping change in the attitudes, approaches and policies of the Government with regard to relations with NGOs and their participation in the government programmes. Besides the Government, the Universities have shown desire to have a much closer interaction with the Community, Civil Society Organizations (CSOs) which include Non-government Organizations (NGOs), Industry, etc. to improve the quality, relevance and efficiency of the academic programmes. Universities are of the opinion that the above agencies are providing apprenticeship/internship training for the students and employing the University graduates in delivering the services to the communities. Now, the disciplines such as Sociology, Social Work, Anthropology, Rural Development, Education/Adult Education, Home Science, Population Studies, etc. have the extension component and doing field outreach activities. The trained graduates from these disciplines are being employed by the Non-governmental Organizations besides the Extension departments of the Government. Some of the established non-governmental organizations are permitting the students to undertake project works, providing apprenticeship internship training and field orientation programmes. Similarly some of the University departments are involved in organizing extension programmes, formulation of developmental programmes, conducting research, documentation of reports and proposal writing and report writing, etc. However, there are no proper guidelines or Memorandum of Understanding for collaboration between Universities and NGOs. No doubt the partnership with NGOs would give an understanding about the changes to be made in the syllabus, approach and methods and to prepare the students with capacities and skills necessary to serve in the voluntary sector.

Features of NGOs

NGOs have a number of distinct features that build upon the foundation for effective collaboration:

1. NGOs are often able to reach segments of rural populations;
2. They engage the poor in capacity building activities as a major component in their programmes and projects;
3. They are recognized for their role in developing new initiatives, new programmes or new approaches, new mechanisms, etc., to address development problems and issues;
4. They possess extensive knowledge of local conditions;
5. NGOs deem active participation by the poor in their development process as an essential pre-condition to their empowerment—participation not only in the implementation of programmes or projects but also in their conceptualization, design, monitoring and evaluation;
6. NGOs can play a significant role in public advocacy, policy analysis and mobilize opinions in support of issues of public concern;
7. NGOs are playing vital role in creating and sustaining the 'Social Capital', i.e. those bonds of trust and reciprocity among people which are essential for democrative society;
8. NGOs are playing the much needed role of capacity building among people and organizations so that rich associations network vibrant enough to take up social and community, building roles, can come to exist.

Socio-Economic Projects Implemented by NGOs

Voluntary organizations are the institutions, which are working at the grassroots level and have undertaken the following projects across the country:

1. Literacy campaigns, NFE programmes, Back to School, Early Childhood Education, Child Labour schools, etc.
2. Health, establishing hospitals with basic services, Health checkup camps, Immunization programmes, Mother and Childcare Services, AIDS Awareness programmes, Nutrition, Family Welfare Planning, Family Counselling services, etc.
3. Organizing Self-Helf Groups, Artisan training, DWACRA groups, thrift campaigns, Income Generation programmes based on appropriate technology.
4. Environmental Protection and Development, Vana Samrakshna Samithies, Plantation and afforestation programmes.
5. Introduction of new cultivation methods, watershed programmes, soil testing services, land reforms, promotion of unions for agriculture labour.
6. Implementation of poverty alleviation programmes such as Jawahar Rojgar Yojana (JRY) Indira Avas Yojana (IAY), Food For Work, Desilting minor irrigation tanks etc.
7. Development of Co-operatives, establishment of Mahila Mandals, youth clubs Old, Age Homes for aged.
8. Mobilization of local resources for community services.
9. Establishing and running of community centers.
10. Promoting communal harmony and national integration.
11. Conducting mass awareness programmes on development activities.
12. Encouraging/Mobilizing people to participate in all development activities.

Collaborative Roles of Universities with the NGOs

Universities have potential to carryout the following roles for the benefit of the NGOs:

(a) *Data Bank:* It is the responsibility of the University to become an effective center for information which is vitally needed for formulation of socio-economic and educational projects needed for the development of deprived communities. Universities are noted for collection, storage and dissemination of information. They supply right and required information to the NGOs for preparing project proposals. It can prepare the Directory of Donor agencies.

(b) *Preparation of Project Proposals:* Universities have expertise in preparation of project proposals based on the guidelines of the doner agencies and interests of the applying NGOs.

(c) *Training:* Initial and Periodic training is needed by the three main categories of functionaries involved in the voluntary organizations viz., promoters, middle level and grassroot level workers. They require proper inputs to enable them to develop knowledge, to develop right/positive attitude and the necessary skills for their effective functioning. Otherwise their efforts are mainly unscientific and fail to yield further results. Here the Universities would play a greater role in organizing the initial training, periodic orientation and refresher courses for the functionaries.

Universities can organize training programmes for the NGO functionaries in all the techniques of extension such as working with the leaders, working with the groups and working through the groups. They may also be trained properly in acquiring a thorough knowledge about the programmes with which they are entrusted. They can also impart skills and capabilities needed for carrying out the functions. Further, they should also get trained in the effective use of communication skills and techniques such as audio-visuals, organizing meetings, rallies, conducting poster campaigns, cultural programmes, etc.

(d) *Consultative Services:* University teachers particularly from the disciplines such as Sociology, Social Work, Home Science, Population, Human Rights, Law, Education, Adult Education have authority to act as consultants for the NGOs which are desirous to solve their problems in a scientific manner. NGOs consult for data, research findings, project proposals, staff recruitment, training, monitoring techniques, evaluation tools, measuring impact of the projects, documentation, etc. Universities with their staff and students visit the rural communities along with the operating NGOs to assess the pros and cons of the programmes which they have undertaken and offer suggestions for effective delivery of services.

(e) *Research and Evaluation:* Universities can undertake the evaluation work of the various programmes organized by the NGOs on their request for improving the delivery of services. They can focus on the following three areas:

- Testing new technologies that have special advantages for the poorest rural people, who are the beneficiaries of developmental projects;
- Testing new institutional approaches in the various sectors and sub-sectors in which the organization is involved to determine their relevance, acceptability and sustainability; and measuring the strengths, weakness, opportunities and threats to the programmes and organizations.

Research should also cover the following four fields:

(1) The effects of socio-economic and developmental programmes on the social environment of rural communities; (2) determination of the necessary social/economic/educational

needs for the campaign against poverty/illiteracy to be successful. (3) Preparation and experimentation of teaching materials/methods/monitoring and evaluation system and (4) Preparation of situation studies and basic socio, economic and cultural needs.

(f) *Reports Writing and Documentation:* Most of the NGO functionaries are engaged in field programmes and are not capable of writing reports and documentation work. Universities can assist the organizations in preparing reports such as periodical Reports, Annual Reports, Final Project Reports, etc. They can also extend help in documenting the work done by the organizations in the process of carrying out the projects and programmes.

(g) *Continuing Professional Education and Lifelong Learning:* Universities can design and implement the Continuing Professional Education Programmes through the part-time or distance education programmes for the enrichment of skills by the functionaries, grassroot level workers and technicians. They can also organize training or re-training classes for the professionals either through weekend or summer classes which offer possibilities for learning and skill development.

Utilisation of Resources of NGOs

The universities can utilize the resources of NGOs for their academic and professional development programmes in the following manner:

(a) Appointing the NGO experts as Adjunct Professors so as to bring the field orientation to the students and exposure to the social service activities. This will help in making the education more relevant to the needs of society.

(b) Nominating the experienced NGO personnel on the Boards of Studies so as to utilize their expertise in designing or re-designing the curriculum of the courses relevant to the social needs.

(c) Identifying the qualified and eligible NGO functionaries and appointing them as supervisors for guiding the regular or distant learners who have undertaken the field-oriented or people-oriented studies so as to bring out the realities in the field.

(d) The field organizations can be used as laboratories for the college/university students to experiment the knowledge which they have gained in the classrooms. These organizations, can provide orientation and apprenticeship training to the students before entering into the world of work.

The Students Role

The Students of College/Universities are expected to participate in the activities of NGOs in different ways:

1. Preparation of reports and theses on the subject of their studies;
2. They will carryout inquiries, sample surveys and statistical studies accompanied with commentaries;
3. They will describe the situation in the different communities where there are highest rates of poverty and illiteracy. These studies should help to adopt the suitable programmes to the special characteristics of the (rural) communities.
4. The students should study other problems such as ill-health, illiteracy, housing, food, etc. Several specific problems such as political, social, aspects relating to girls, child labour, migrants and adults in general will also be studied.
5. Students could prepare advertising posters, organize press campaigns, etc.

Collaborative Roles of NGOs with Universities

NGOs in turn have to contribute the following for Universities to improve the quality of education and effective delivery of services to the poorer sections of the society.

(a) *Become the Laboratories for the Students*

- Allow the students to undertake project works, provide apprenticeship training, internship and field orientation programmes etc. in the areas of operation;
- Invite the staff and students to their projects to assess the functioning of the field programmes and to the functions, annual days and special days that they celebrate so as to understand the field problems, gain experience and develop positive attitude towards voluntary sector.

(b) *Facilitate for Earn while Learn Programme*

- Recruit the students with social service background on part-time basis by the organizations which are accessible to the campuses to induce motivation, aptitude and develop work culture among them.

(c) *Contribute for Quality Education*

- Serve on the boards of studies to design or re-design the curriculum suitable to meet the requirements of the field-oriented courses.
- The Chief Executives and the Administrators can serve as Adjunct professors and share their experiences in the social service departments of the Universities.

Role of NGOs on the Campuses of Colleges/Universities

The NGOs can also adopt the schemes sanctioned by the UGC or State Government particularly under Xth Plan for effective implementation:

- Maintenance of University Hostels for better quality and the universities are eased with the hostel administration and they can concentrate on academic activities;
- Organize Day Care Centers where all the teachers and employees can bring their children which will facilitate the persons particularly women to continue the academic and administrative careers;

- Conduct Remedial Coaching centers for disadvantaged sections of the society such as SC/ST, Minorities and disabled persons. These centers enable the students to bridge the gap resulting from their earlier education and social deprivation.
- Provide proper infrastructural facilities such as toilets, drinking water, communication facilities, recreation, parking etc., for staff and students. Further, provide facilities for differently abled persons to enable them to access the class rooms, laborataries, toilets, etc.

Suggestions for Selecting the Suitable NGOs for Collaboration

The following basic criteria may be suggestive for selecting the NGOs for collaboration:

- Substantial experience in working with the rural poor and with the specific project activities;
- The technical capacity to perform the tasks at hand;
- Accountability to its partners, particularly project beneficiaries;
- The financial capacity to receive, manage and monitor funds;
- Availability of adequate management and qualified field staff;
- Knowledge of the local situation and access to target communities;
- The ability to be innovative and adaptable;
- Adoption of participatory methodologies and tools;
- The readiness to place its operations in the context of community plans, local authority plans and national government plans; and
- A long-term commitment to—and emphasis on—sustainability.

Further, care must be taken to select an NGO as a partner:

- The NGOs must be registered in accordance with relevant laws as a non-profit-making organization;

- Priority is given to local NGOs and local branches of national or international NGOs working in close connection with local communities.
- Avoid the NGOs which duplicate private enterprises.

Conclusion

Universities have to take initiation in identifying the suitable non-governmental organizations for better collaboration in the matters of quality education for the students in developing right attitude among the students and staff towards social service activities, designing suitable projects for the deprived communities, conducting research and evaluation of projects, etc., with the NGOs. The NGOs should also extend their cooperation in training the students, sharing their experiences, providing placement to the students either on part-time or full-time basis so that the social service activities will be expanded for the upliftment of the resource depiived communities.

14

Products of Universities vis-à-vis Mission of NGOs

M. Ramaswamy

Non-Government Organizations (or voluntary organisations as they exist) generally enter those fields which are either neglected or ill-served by Govt. agencies. NGOs shape their services with a missionary zeal. An ideal NGOs single-minded objective is to serve the society without expecting any return-without regard for reward, recognition or remuneration. The way University education is shaped, as a rule, to impart knowledge of a particular field. Book learning alone will not ensure that justice will be given to their profession. Students have to be imbibed with human considerations and value system, so that they will rise to higher levels of thinking. Their knowledge then will be directed to improve the lot of sections they will be serving. Students coming out of University will immediately look for security in the form of employment or self-employment. They try to sell themselves! Their efforts during study are treated as investment for their own future prosperity. With this outlook how can they fit into the philosophy of NGOs? When students enter the portal of University, they should feel that it is an opportunity to become useful citizens of the country. If they are self-centred how can the nation progress? The aberrations occur when one forgets that the "atma" is the most important component of a human being. Education must cater equally and in balanced proportion to the needs of the body mind and soul but not merely the Head! Education must have a strong moral and spiritual slant. But that does not mean academic work is relegated to secondary status. In our country, which has a rich heritage, human development should be top priority in University. If the values are abandoned, it would be the death knell of civilised society. Until about fifty years ago, educational establishments everywhere regarded character development and training students to be good citizens as very high in the list of priorities. Lately, however the stress has shifted almost exclusively to imparting wordly skills. When values cease to have any place in the scheme of things, society ends up paying a heavy price. Indeed a good fraction of the crime today is committed by intelligent and college educated people as should be evident from the 'number of corporate frauds, cyber-crimes and high level corruption.

The primary motive in today's world behind taking up a job is money. Here lies the difference between NGOs (or voluntary organisations) and Govt. agencies. The latter is bound by rules, which are time bound and targets bound. The mission with which NGOs toil is absent in Govt. departments. Here lies the need for University to prepare the students to accept challenges which NGOs are taking up. There appears to be a shift in emphasis in the very objective of education. Instead of being a moral and social obligation and an instrument of man-making education, specially higher education, has become a mode of investment. Leap frog into modern technology may show some immediate results but cannot show sustainable development. It may also fall as a whimper! There is a growing apprehension that in this storm of technological boom, human development is a casualty. Key issues— poverty, health, education are being sidelined. It is felt that higher education is concerned with marketable courses and their employment potential. What is the role of higher education in this setting? Is there adequate concern for farming and non-farming needs of rural India? What is the impact of technology on the poverty and human development? Is their sufficient stress on values in higher education? Basically, is the country, the core formed by rural India, ready to receive the type of technology related jobs? The twentieth century has been described as age of science and technology. The present century might well be information age, knowledge-age or the age of genetic design. Progress means increase in wealth and standard of living. In the process importance of values appear to have been overlooked. A thousand years ago this land gave humanity the treasure of ultimate bliss and happiness. Should India seek mere IT super-power status or lead this world in this hour of moral darkness?

15

Role of Universities in Building a Strong NGOs through Human Resources

An Innovative Experiment

K. Prabhakar
K. Penchalaiah
J.G. Thirupal
A. Paparao

Non-governmental Organisations (NGOs) have emerged as an important element of contemporary Indian Society. They have been variously described as the third sector, civil society, non-profits, voluntary sector etc. NGOs which by their nomenclature do not appear part of any government policy or programme, and actually supported and promoted by governments. These are registered bodies and are allowed to function under certain rules and regulations. There are given support by various governments especially to take up the issues which according to governments are of prime concern for the society to develop but where government, due to variety of reasons, have failed to develop appropriate systems to tackle handle. Due to their active involvement in the areas where government initiatives are lacking or not appropriate or limited, many NGOs have got credential position among their clientele, most of them poor and deprived. NGOs are engaged in the issues related to women and child development, health and medical and programmes rural infrastructure development, self development programmes etc. So NGOs are considered as third sector which helps in making a strong nation.

On the other hand, universities are playing a primary role in producing young graduates and postgraduates especially from social sciences which are major sources for NGOs. In this context, an attampt is to discuss how universities help on building a strong NGOs through Human Resources.

NGOs in India

The voluntary action is not a new one. It has a long history. In India its history is closely associated with the history of democratic struggle. In early eighteenth century, voluntary action was carried out by great Indians like Raja Rammohan Rai, Ishwar Chandra Vidyasagar, Keshab Chandra Sen, M.G. Ranade, Telang, Phule, Pandite Rambai, Annie Besant and many others. Many of them formed groups or associations. Some of these were Brahma Samaj (1828), Pavanhansa Sabha (1849), Sarvajanik Sabha (1871), Prarthana Samaj (1862), Arya Samaj (1875), Widow Marriage Association (1850), Arya Mahila Samaj (1868), Ramakrishna Mission (1897), Theosophical Society, Indian, National Congress (1885), and the Indian Social Conference (1897). These were formed mainly to bring about change and reform in various aspects of social life.

Till the end of nineteenth century, voluntary services however, remained the domain of the volunteers and they started working through organised groups and agencies because of the complexities of problems and change in situation. After independence, government recognized the importance of NGOs in developing our nation. This result in rapid growth of funding for NGOs by government and external donors. As for as the government funding is concerned, there are over 200 government schemes initiated by the central and state government through which NGOs can have direct access to resources for rural development. At the district level, there are over 300 schemes and programmes in which NGOs could involve them and felicitate the flow of resources in favour of the poor. A rough estimate reveals that more than 1.2 million (12 lakhs) NGOs exists in India. According to Ministry of Home Affairs, in 1985-86 there were only 7000 voluntary organisations under FCRA account, which have increased more than three-fold to 22924 in 2001. The capital city of Delhi alone has more than 84000 registered societies under the Society Registration Act (1860). There are other acts like the Indian Trust Act (1882), Charitable Companies Act (1950), the Indian Companies Act, (1985) under article 25, the Cooperative Society Act (1904) under which charitable trusts or non-profit institutions can be registered. Besides these, there are large proportions of voluntary social formations which are non-registered and also very active in local governance. The logic for growing voluntary sector in India are also often traced to favorable government policy since Seventh Five Year Plan, and the process of liberalization and globalization that has increased penetration of foreign resources directly to the voluntary organisation.

NGOs and Human Resources

Human Resources are taken as most crucial and complex resources in an organisation and it is an empirically well established fact that in to-days competitive world, it is a crucial resources adding competitive advantage to the organization. Human resources is also a valuable resources in the NGO. Which is a fully people-driven organization. The sustained and continuous success of NGOs would depend efficient Human Resources/Volunteers.

Volunteers /Human Resources help in:

- Development or partnership between the organisation and the people among whom they work.
- Filling same of gaps in the statutory services and making services available to the people.
- Promoting harmonious and functional relationships.
- Assisting individuals, groups and communities in understanding and analysing their problems and thereby arriving at certain solutions.
- Reducing the sufferings of the sick, handicapped and mentally ill persons.

- Liaisoning between the persons in need of services and other resource groups who can help is dealing with the problem of the needy.
- They can also occasionally function as pressure group by drawing attention to unmet needs and peers for effective action.
- It is observed that most of the NGOs in India are suffering enormously due to lack of efficient leadership by founders of social workers and improper cooperation between volunteers. A wide range of problems are faced by volunteers in the course of their work.
- Many of the volunteers do not have the required skills and they also do not have time to gain understanding and learn skills. These result in limiting their achievements and, thereby increasing their frustration.
- Lack of proper command over the language of poor communication of the group/individual among whom are is expected to work.
- Lack of proper planning or non-involvement result in poor implementation of the programme.
- Lack of proper guidance consequently remain ignorant about the totality of the programme.
- Many volunteers have appointed without proper training.

NGOs and Universities

Universities are the centers of producing human resources required for the society. Many graduates and post-graduates of especially social sciences are interested in joining third sectors i.e., NGOs .Hence, there is urgent need to search for ways and means of creating new kinds of linkage between universities and NGOs in order to initiate and motivate the young volunteers in joining NGOs.

Traditionally, Universities are encouraging technical and professional education which have placement in various corporate, profit-oriented organisations and scientific labs. Universities have to redefine the importances of NGOs in developing a strong nation. The following are suggestions to motivate and encourage the young graduates and post-graduates in joining the NGOs.

1. Universities have to arrange campus placements by offering many NGOs.
2. Universities are to arrange seminars, conferences, and workshops on NGOs can give initial awareness.
3. Giving permissions to various NGOs for stimulating and conducting various training programmes can develop skills is volunteers.
4. Providing various counseling and consultants services to the needy ones how to join NGOs its functions and performing other procedural activities.
5. Universities have to introduce diplomas, certificates courses etc on NGOs.
6. Universities have to introduce lessons on NGOs in the curriculum of social sciences.
7. Universities has to supply various successful stirs of NGOs to social science students.
8. Professors of social sciences have to encourage young scholars to preserve research in NGOs.

Conclusion

Keeping in view above mentioned scenario, it can be concluded that volunteerism which is an important ingredient of democracy will sustain, nourish and strengthen the economy of the country. Universities and the government has to come forward in encouraging young people to comes the hallmarks of creativities, energy adventure and idealism in developing volunteerism.

No doubt, young people the world over are creative and energetic, committed and idealistic and have no vested interests to protect. And to think the India has nearly 40 million of them perhaps, no other asset could be more precious.

REFERENCES

1. Rajesh Tandor , "Volunteerism in Indian Today" Yojana Dec, 2001.
2. Pankaj, Naithani,'NGOs Rural Development' *Kurukshetra*, Sept, 2001.
3. D. Rajasekhar, "Non-Governmental Organisations in India: Opportunities and Challenges" Institutes of Social and Economic Change, Bangalore, 2002.

Theme III

Review and Updating of the Curriculum of PG and Diploma Courses

16

Review and Updating of the Curriculum

G.V.R.R Prasad

The present system of education is far from meeting the requirements and realities of life and livelihood of an individual. The present day human society is undergoing radical changes, the fundamental problems of human relationships, and values, the requirements of economic development are becoming increasingly insoluble, and people are looking (turning) towards education for a suitable and possible means of practical remedies. But unfortunately the present aims, methods and contents of education do not act upon or address themselves to these problems. Moreover the common man cannot bear the increasing costs of education. If education continues to be what it is today, the issues of human development, human destiny and human fulfillment, the new directions and goals that seen impossible of achievement. Therefore education can be conceived as a methodized organization of life.

It is generally agreed that the educational needs and demands of rural India have not received proper attention, despite certain popular schemes which have brought about salutary changes in certain aspects. Still human potential in the rural India has remained untapped. So the immediate needs is that suitable teaching and learning material have to be so designed that they are relevant to the rural environment and ethos. The technical knowhow, which needs to be transferred to the rural areas has to be judiciously determined. Scientific and technical knowledge regarding alternative and non-conventional sources of energy must receive highest priority in the educational programmes. Rural employment schemes must be linked with specially designed relevant programmes of education for rural youth (example— Agro-industrial complexes) so that there should be a growing demand for the relevant talent and skills, which in term, should impose a new trend or dimension to education. Rural employment schemes must also be linked with specially designed relevant programmes of education.

During the last five years education sector has gone many changes. A good number of new courses have been started. The changes that took place in the field of science and technology and production have been reflected in the education sector. Due to globalization, the changes that occur in other countries are showing their effect in our country also. We have two different sections in education sector. One is pertaining to new courses, latest equipments with conveniently arranged educational institutions which involves huge capital investments (corporate sector) another is with ordinary courses, consisting poor infrastructural facilities and amenities. The first one is accessable only to the elite and rich people, and the poor and middle class can have access in the ill-equiped educational institutions with poor infrastructure facilities. Hence the objective of providing equal opportunities of education to the people has not been fulfilled as such the gap between rich and poor becoming wide. Various reports on education such as CABE reveals the fact of poor infrastructural facilities and the plight of education in our country. It is very painful to note that only 8.9 per cent youth in the age group of 17 to 23 are studying higher education. This figure is still high even in Srilanka and Bangladesh. In developed countries 80 per cent of youth in the same age group are studying higher education. Our rulers, planners and educational administrators are repeatedly telling that a knowledge society will be created soon, but no suitable steps in that direction are taking place. The Govt. (Central) have constituted certain committees to study the reasons why the number of students in higher education are comparatively very less.

The CABE sub committee under the chairmanship of Prof. Mungekar have stated that due to high fee structure many students do not have access to higher education, and further expressed that, the fees collected in our country is very high when compared to other developed countries. The committee further stated that the level of privatization of education in our country is very high than in any other country except in Japan and South Korea. The above sub-committee of CABE have also suggested that the Govt. should control the high level of fee collection in educational institutions and provide more budget for education in the country. The "Kothari Commission" (1964) have suggested that 6 per cent of GDP should spent on education. But this was not been implemented. If we take this recommendation into consideration the Central and State Govts. put together have to incur expenditure of Rs. 1,67,000 crores on education. But only Rs. 97,000 crores have been incurred expenditure on education. Hence, it is very clear that unless the Govts. increase the expenditure on education it is not possible to provide higher education to all. The policy of privatizing higher education will not help the poor in any way, because the private institutions will collect more fee which the poor cannot pay. The judgment of Supreme Court in the case of T.M. Pai, that the Govt. should not have control on private educational institutions may cause more damage to the policy of reservations to poor, merit may not be recognized for admission, high fee collection and less talented teachers may take place, which will hamper the objectives of education. Keeping this in view if necessary, the Govt. may effect constitutional amendments, so as to enable the courts to give proper judgements, and to plug the holes wherever necessary.

Another dangerous dimension of education is that, making educational policies suitable and helpful to meet the needs of developed countries, our educational policies are giving such impression that study in foreign universities and educational institutions is more prestigious. The proposed four year degree course can be seen as a part of above policy. We should have proper plan of desiring and implementing our own indigenous education suitable to our needs and requirements.

Educational reconstruction should necessitate certain fundamental innovations such as—Review and re-determination of the constants of education in the light of the emerging needs of synthesis of knowledge and culture, as also of increasing demands of scientific and technological skills, promotion of values, and integral development of personality. Lightening the burden of books. Changes in the methodology of education so as to meet the total needs of the cognitive effective and co native growth of students.

Radical changes in the examination system so as to achieve the goal of de-linking of degrees from jobs and to develop national tests that would be both objective and reliable and would test not only competence in a few selected subjects, but also achievements in the fields of value-oriented education, physical fitness, skills for specific personality. Development of culture of educational innovation and experimentation directly related to the emerging demands of the 21st century.

Research is indispensable not only for attaining educational excellence but also for securing higher rate of economic growth, productivity, and development. Hence high priority should be assigned to the promotion of research, both scientific and humanistic.

Just two and half decades ago, we had thought of by building a new structure of education under 10 + 2 + 3 pattern and with a bit of physical education, socially useful work experience, three languages, value education, so as to be in conformity with scientific education. We would have given to the country all that is needed educationally. But just within a decade, it was found that vocational education, which was the main attraction of the new pattern, could not flourish, and the three language formula is still remain unimplemented in several parts of the country, and the claims of ancient languages like Sanskrit and Tamil still remain unfulfilled. Physical education has hardly developed. The burden of books has increased. The burden of entrance tests at every terminal point is bothering students even at the highest level of their development. And demands are being made to find new ways and means by which our curricula are reformulated and the examination system completely overhauled. Regarding revision of the current curricula the considerations would be:

- The load of books should be reduced to the optimum level.
- Appropriate to every terminal point, two years vocational courses should be made available to every student who wants to opt for them.
- The requirements of the target groups—their capacity to absorb the messages contained in the curricula, should be kept in view.
- The curricula should be three types. (a) Introductory (b) General knowledge type and (c) Specialized knowledge type—the purpose being to allow students to pursue various curricula according to their interests and talents and also according to the careers that they want to choose in their life.
- In the context of changing knowledge, expanding frontiers of knowledge should be brought through constant curricular changes nearer to students as quickly as possible and efforts should be made to frame curricula in such a manner that it is easy for students to make the distinction between the essential and the non-essential, central and peripheral, useful and not so-useful.
- More emphasis should be laid on linguistic competence so that as the student advances, his or her capacities of expression in the medium of education as also in their languages will be improved.
- Many problems of constant enrichment arise because of the deficiencies of the curricula and of the available teaching learning material.

We should note that at present there is no machinery in our country through which curricular changes can be brought about. Therefore it would be necessary to establish assemblies of experts in different parts of the country as also a coordinating body at the national level as permanent bodies charged with the responsibilities connected with the curricular changes required.

Curricular changes necessarily demand new teaching and learning materials, which in term will have to be specially designed in view of the fact that new methodologies of education, including those of T.V and Computer will required new styles of presentation. Appropriate agencies for this purpose should also be created at local, regional and national levels.

REFERENCES

1. *Education At Cross Roads*, by Kireet Joshi Published by the Mother's Institute of Research 2000.

2. "Videsi Dasyam Disaga Vidya" by R. Arun Kumar Published in *Vaartha* Telugu Daily page 4. dt. 15/11/2005.

3. Report of the Committee for Review of NPE 1986 by Govt. of India.

17

Review and Updating the Curriculum of Post-Graduate and Diploma Courses from Adult to Lifelong Learning

Rajesh, J.K. Dixit

The University Grants Commission in its policy framework recognized extension as third dimension of the university—system. It has been accorded the same status like teaching and research which are the traditional role of higher education. This recognition has redefined the role of universities and incorporated the concept of social commitment and social relevance aspect of higher education system. To operationalise this concept, the universities were encouraged to set up cells/ centers of Adult, Continuing Education and Extension throughout the country in 1978 onwards. This period matched with the launch of National Adult Education program by Government of India. The size and scale of this program for India necessitated the active involvement of the institutions of higher learning which are endowed with educated manpower and knowledge resource. The high ideals of Adult Education program in developed countries like liberation of human being, humanistic approach etc. led to the concept of lifelong learning. Right from the International Conference on Adult Education held in Elsinore (Denmark) in 1949 to the Tokyo Conference (1972-73), the concept of lifelong education became well established. The participating countries were expected to gear the entire education policies and programs around lifelong learning. Educational planners, government representatives and adult educationists arrived at consensus to give the concept of lifelong learning a pivot to all educational activities.

In every contemporary society, the Adult Education in one form or the other has always been there. But the later period of the last century witnessed the institutionalization of this academic exercise. The advocacy on behalf of the educationists and philosophers as well as the demand created through them put tremendous pressure to set up distinct institutions for this specific purpose. The non-formal system of education was also accorded significant status like formal system of education. The changing role of education for the development of individual and in turn the entire society, also became imperative to impart education to those who were not enrolled in any formal educational system.

Adult Education as one of the distinct academic endeavour was recognized by the Government of India in late 1970s. Sporadic and local efforts were made by various local government, agencies and individuals in the past. Some of them were successful and others weathered away with the passage of time. The role of institutions of higher learning were recognized as inevitable in fulfillment of this national goal. During initial phases of this program, the role assigned to universities and colleges were limited. The students were expected to volunteer themselves for imparting literacy skill in the community. This was called center based approach in which illiterate people in the community were enrolled and taught by the volunteer instructors. The instructors were mostly drawn from colleges. The Departments of Adult and Continuing Education were expected to impart training to these instructors and motivate them to take up this task. Gradually this experiment weaned away because of various reasons. The thrust of the policies and programs in this area has also been changing in the successive five-year plans. Gradually the role of the universities in this particular area of social development became more focused which was diffused earlier. At academic level, it was felt that the issue of adult education is a bigger one and literacy is only-one component of it. The concept of lifelong learning is intimately connected with adult education. This area is rather interdisciplinary and multidisciplinary. The concept of life learning also warrant the expansion of these centers/ departments in the university-system with strong academic base. The initial academic programs in the form of diplomas and P. G. diplomas were also initiated in various universities along with the various extension activities. Some of these programs like Post M. A. Diploma in Adult and Continuing Education was given priority in selection of teachers in District Institutes of Education and Training (DIET) and Directorate of Adult Education under the Ministry of Human Resource Development. Various short-term need based courses were also initiated by universities to cater to the need of institutional and external clientele etc. These academic efforts must have served their purpose up to some extent.

In the contemporary world where globalization and liberalization of economy are not the mere slogan, but reality, the restructuring of all the institutions have become imperative. The advancement of technology particularly in the communication sector makes it possible to obtain all kinds of information in a jiffy. The modern age which may be called the "information age" and the society a "Knowledge Society" call upon the education system and particularly the higher education to pause and ponder. The right to information also demands the system of higher education to remodel itself to suit the need of contemporary society.

The establishment of centers/departments of Adult and Continuing Education was institutional necessity, but the status and recognition due to it was not accorded. The traditional role and thinking of the system did not allow it to grow properly. This department because marginalized in the university system. The traditional mindset recognizes the traditional role of teaching and research. In this backdrop, the departments of Adult and Continuing Education will have to change themselves. In absence of the strong academic and research program, the justification for due recognition will become in vain.

It will have to be accepted that these departments are interdisciplinary where personnel from all the disciplines have been working. The field experience and running of various courses have given adequate academic raw material to build up a distinct edifice of its own. The rudimentary research activities can become refined and widened in the mould of established social science research models.

The investigators have tried to express their opinion on the basis of experiences gained so far by working in this area for quite sometime. There is a strong need to replace adult education with lifelong learning which is a established concept throughout the world. The UOC should also be convinced to accept this terminology for all its purposes. There is a need to start postgraduate program on the basis of the concept of lifelong learning. The emerging areas like environmental education, disaster management, gerontology, energy, women and tribal issues are some of the areas, which must find its place in the curriculum. The fundamentals of lifelong learning, research methodology, human resource development, management of social development programs along with population education and counselling are other areas. The existing faculty must be trained to specialize in the area of their interest to take up the responsibility of teaching. The research program should also be strengthened to develop scholarship. The short-term courses, which are need based, should be developed for institutional and community level. The admission criterion for short-term courses should be flexible. They should be non-credit and non-evaluative and self-supporting. The department should run as much short-term courses as possible and rest of the courses can be conducted by NGOs for which technical resource support can be provided by the department. This department can also take up the role of training for non-governmental organizations working in the are of social development. The UGC must support these departments in terms of providing adequate resources including teaching positions. A clear-cut mandate should be given by the UGC to all the universities to consider this department as a nodal center for all the extension activities. In this way, these departments can improve their status and recognition along with clear path of development in future.

The Twenty-Five years of the history of extension education in the university-system (1980-2005) helped in institutionalizing extension education in 73 universities of India by 2005. The focus of the adult education center/department changed from time to time with the development of the universe of knowledge. Several milestones in this field demonstrated the development in this field from Adult Education to Lifelong Learning. The UGC under its reviews of Xth Plan should consider restructuring of these Departments/Centres as the Departments of Lifelong Learning, which automatically assimilates the components of continuing, non-formal and the interests of the non-literates. In course of time the focus of literacy and post-literacy have changed in form of Continuing Education in both developing and developed countries. Thus the Lifelong Learning Department of the university-system will focus its roles and responsibilities in terms of developing short and long term courses pertaining to newer social development areas designing, training-curriculum, identifying and undertaking field-based action research which has the direct relevance with the society. It should also design linkages specifically with business and industry which would include work ethics work-culture for the changing world of work.

The lifelong Learning Department will cater to the needs of the adolescents, youth, older people, vulnerable and marginalized groups especially women, SC/ST population who are living below the poverty line.

REFERENCES

1. Rajesh (2002), Extension Educatin Challenges, Priorities and Lesson Learnt, *Indian Journal of Adult Education*. July-September, 63.
2. UGC, (2002) Xth Plan Guidelines on Adult, Continuing Education, Extension and Field outreach, New Delhi : Univeristy Grants Commission.

The Twenty Five years of the history of extension education in the university system 1980–2005 helped in institutionalizing extension education in 73 universities of India by 2005. The focus of the adult education centres/department changed from time to time with the development of the universe of knowledge. Several milestones in this field demonstrated the development in this field from Adult Education to Lifelong Learning. The UGC under its reviews of Xth Plan should consider restructuring of these Departments/Centres as the Departments of Lifelong Learning which automatically assimilates the components of continuing, non-formal and the interests of the non-literates. In course of time the focus of literacy and post literacy have changed to form of Continuing Education in both developing and developed countries. Thus the Lifelong Learning Departments of the university system will focus its roles and responsibilities in terms of developing short and long term courses pertaining to other social development areas, designing training curriculum, identifying and undertaking field based action research which has the direct relevance with the society. It should also design linkages specifically with business and industry which would include work ethics work culture for the changing world of work.

The lifelong Learning Department will cater to the needs of the adolescents, youth, older people, vulnerable and marginalized groups especially women, SC/ST population who are living below the poverty line.

REFERENCES

1. Rajesh. 2002. Extension Education: Challenges, Priorities and Lessons Learnt. *Indian Journal of Adult Education*. Jul.-September. 63.

2. UGC. 2002. XI Plan Guidelines on Adult, Continuing Education, Extension and Field outreach. New Delhi: University Grants Commission.

Theme IV

Integrated Development: Role of NGOs and Universities

18

Role of NGOs and Universities in Integrated Development Process

P. Adinarayana Reddy
D. Uma Devi

Integrated Development

Development is a broad concept which also embraces growth. It covers both qualitative and quantitative aspects and is multidimensional in nature. It affects the qualitative changes in social, economic, political, cultural, environmental aspects, in other words, overall development of an area in general and individual. In particular further Development is a continuous and unending process, aiming at immediate improvement of the living conditions of the people or increase the potential for betterment of living conditions in future. Development is a function of several disciplines and always is an integrated one. In the integrated development, though the economic development aspired much, cannot be separated from the social, cultural, environmental aspects.

The integrated development involves different categories of integrations such as special integration (integration between areas, integration of different sectors with forward and backward linkages), integration of economic development with social development, integration of total area approach with target group approach, integration of credit with technical service, integration of human resource development with manpower needs by dovetailing education and training programmes with anticipated manpower needs, health, water supply, nutrition, education, training, income generating programmes etc.

Role of NGOs

The task of integrated development is a multifaceted one which requires multi-disciplinary approach. The failure of the Government in reaching the downtrodden and effective implementation of the developmental programmes initiated by the Government has paved a way for alternative agencies viz., Non-Governmental Organizations (NGOs). The Non-Governmental Organizations are effective in their approach because of their simplicity, autonomous, commitment, who can easily acclimatize themselves to the local problems and requirements and work as a catalyst of change and development. They are quite suited to serve as effective intermediaries between the target (beneficiaries) and Government and bring about awareness and motivate the people for a better life by availing the facilities from different sources. The NGOs are involved in the areas of education, training, welfare, skill development, income-generation, old age physically handicapped welfare, and what not in every aspect of the development process, are functioning effectively.

In other words, the NGOs are involved in all spheres of the life of an individual starting from womb to tomb. NGOs apart from the Government, is one of the biggest network covering all sections of the population in the society. The NGOs can play a lead role in educating the community about its culture and tradition enabling it to enrich and transmit the same to the future generations. In addition, it can also educate the community about the various avenues and opportunities created by the Government in the form of developmental programmes for their welfare and development and empower the people to demand for their share.

No doubt, the NGOs too have inherited problems of recognization from the community and the Government. The community will recognize the institutions only if they believe that these institutions will solve their problems and assist them in difficult situations. Once the community recognizes the services of the agency, the community will blindly follow the directions of the NGOs.

In view of the recognization from the community, the agencies with the assistance of Government can undertake the integrated programmes rather than isolated programmes at the community level. These agencies should create awareness among the community about the importance of the education in individual development and the overall development of the community as a whole. Further, they can take up the programmes to create awareness about the various developmental programmes initiated by the Government for various groups enabling them to utilize the opportunities. A number of agencies are providing specialized services to the community and this information will enable the community to make use of the services effectively.

Role of Universities

In the process of integrated development of the individual and thereby the society, the universities can play a vital role in creating awareness, development of aptitude and bringing change in the attitude of the people. The universities are the social institutions created to promote and develop the required skills and knowledge leading to the promotion of human resources. Further, universities facilitates for promoting the new innovations through its research activities. These innovations are relevant and useful to the common people and disseminates them through its extension activities. Recognizing the value of extension, the universities are recognized it as its third dimension. Hence, there are extension wings of various disciplines, which were created to organize various activities in the community to inculcate the awareness among the people to empower them to attain the socio-economic development. It is now widely accepted that literacy paves the way for the development of an individual and thereby the development of the community and a nation as a whole.

University as an apex institution, can create an educative environment for promotion of literacy which can pave a way for development among the community, can promote an urge among the people for further education and development. Universities can promote and shape the values among various sections of the people through curriculum, initiatives on campus, partnerships and mentorship programmes developed in collaboration with other educational institutions, businesses and local communities. It helps the students in acquiring and developing the skills and competencies such as social, employable, real life experiences, communication and co-operation, new knowledge and perspectives, knowledge and expertise within the trans-disciplinary research, and able to connect the various needs and demands of different groups with their theoretical and scientific background etc.

Universities have an advantage over other institutions to explore, experiment and communicate complex and sometimes controversial social issues. They have the opportunity and ability to engage in interdisciplinary research and practices and learn how to deal with complex, non-linear systems that characterize social and environmental challenges prevailing in the society. However, the universities created for the above could not discharge their responsibilities effectively. The reasons are many and also different.

Suggestions

Keeping in view of the role of NGOs and universities in the Integrated Development process, the following suggestions were made to acclimatize themselves to suit to the demanding needs. They are:

1. Both the NGOs and Universities should go together to find out the problems and needs of the society.
2. Universities should concentrate and promote on the action research activities which are helpful for the integrated development of the society.
3. The Universities should also disseminate its innovations which will be helpful for the development process through its extension departments.

4. The NGOs should take initiation to disseminate the University's innovations and activities which will help in development process.

5. The NGOs and Universities should have linkages to meet the problems and demands of the society as well as to equip the students to build their future career.

6. The NGOs and Universities should work together to create gender biased, gender sensitive society by inculcating awareness among the people about their rights, duties, responsibilities towards the nation and the society.

7. They should go together not only in creating awareness, they should also motivate the people for the effective community participation in the developmental process.

8. The Universities should take initiation to find out the problems of the NGOs in their work and should try to suggest overcome them.

9. The Universities should also take initiation to consider the recommendations and suggestions of the NGOs in equipping its students to fulfill the demands and career requirements of the NGOs so as to enable them to work effectively.

10. The Universities should organize the seminars and conferences, discussions etc., with both the NGOs and administrators for their collaboration and co-operation in taking the developmental initiatives.

11. The curriculum of the Universities should be re-structured according to the present context and practical utility in the field with field experiences and other practical works.

12. Community based research centres should be established as a mandatory part of Universities.

13. The NGOs before planning their programmes should collect baseline data as well as make an effort to understand the socio-cultural aspects of the people among whom they are working.

The Universities should provide consultancy services to the NGOs in promoting the quality of work in the developmental process.

19

Integrated Development
Role of Universities and NGOs

K. Sudha Rani
G. Hussain Reddy

Development has been a paramount concern of both the Government and Non-Governmental Organisations for many decades. A series of approaches and strategies have been developed and used for integrated development. These efforts have made different amount of dent on the development of people in the society. Most of these development initiatives have been undertaken in a vary segmented manner. For example, technical training courses have been directed towards equiping students with occupational skills in areas offering limited employment potential Agricultural extension workers have promoted the growing of crops for which there is no market. The main reason for this is lack of co-ordination between the government departments, Ministries, NGO's and field level workers. In this context an attempt has been made by the author to study role of Universities and NGOs in the integrated development of the society and suggested few measures to bridge the gap between the efforts of the Universities and NGOs.

Role of Universities

It has become increasingly evident that Universities in developing countries are accepted as instruments of change charged with the mandate to produce trained manpower, the education of good citizens, and as centres for the advancement and accumulation of knowledge. As an instrument of change, a university pursues knowledge for the service of society and this spirit in inculcated into its teaching, research and public service or outreach functions. It has also been accepted that each of these three functions should support one another, so that decisions about any one of the traditional academic programmes geared to the development of high level manpower to serve the growing nation and the discovery or creation of better ways of doing things, the institution must see that its expertise as well as new knowledge is extended to the outside community. A University is obliged to step out into the main currents of life, actively seeking among the people to discover and help define their problems. Designing and management of a systematic mechanism would be the base of the University for supporting the rural people. The factors influence the management mechanisms that may be instituted to support a universities outreach function are as follows:

University Out Reach Goals

A clear set of outreach goals will certainly be very useful to a University so that it can allocate its resources accordingly. At the same time, it must also set its future goals for outreach. With these present and future goals clearly identified, the university can identify the transformations it must take in order to achieve the future goals.

Staff Commitment

In order to conduct outreach activities effectively, a University really needs to maximise the effective use of faculty time and expertise. University outreach activities require travel and depend a lot on clientele demands for certain knowledge and services. The expertise and academic talents of a University will be found in the various academic departments. It is necessary to establish viable linkages with these academic departments that are effectively coordinated to support and backstop a particular outreach activity.

Financial Allocation

A university will have to judiciously manage and allocate its financial resources for its various functions. There are several major financial items for a public service outfit. First is the initial investment layout and equipment. Second is the need for staff and a sizeable operating budget.

External Linkage

Linkages to be created can thus be categorised into two, either as internal linkages or as external linkages. Internally, the various disciplines can work together on a common problem faced by the rural people. In linking externally, the mechanism may perhaps be through, or with the organisations and individuals that the University associates with such as other research or development agencies. The University can play four roles in the area of community development include following.

1. *Piloting of New Strategies and Approaches*

In disciplines where it has expertise and resources the University can initiate and carryout the pilot projects on new strategies and approaches. It can be done by two ways. One is where the University conducts by itself, controlling certain treatments to assess the impact of one or several factors. Another type of pilot projects with one or several other agencies which are all interested.

2. *Supporting Training*

Many government agencies and NGOs may have their own training programmes. However, they may not be able to cover all aspects or all levels of their personnel. This is where the University can helpful in the gap by complementing the training programme that it can best provide.

3. *Creation and Production Support Materials*

Another major role is in the creation and production of support material that have the knowledge bases in the academic disciplines of the University. Many implementing agencies do not have the necessary resources to sustain this creative activity, that has to depend on new ideas and findings.

4. *Advisory or Consultancy*

University experts can offer their advice for the benefit of planning, research, implementation and other ongoing activities of various public, individuals or organisations.

A priority concern is for the University to convince the public of its noble intentions in conducting outreach. This university philosophy must be understood because it supports the search for both relevance and excellence in its disciplines. Pilot project examples must be accepted as justifiable University activities which consequently require the procurement of funding. The University should, however, ensure that the staff resources do not neglect primary university duties.

The university also need to support the institutionalisation of support training, materials production and the advisory roles. This is necessary in order that the universities resources can be best used, and external demands be coordinated and thus produced an appropriate university response. The mechanics of accomplishing this may differ from campus to campus, but the basic steps include the following. First, there is the provision by the University of a substantial development and operation budget to conduct such programmes. Although these functions may self-supporting in the long-run, the initial funding for an office and equipment can be quite substantial. Secondly a mechanism must be established in the university to oversee as well as administer these programmes, that are subjected to periodic policy reviews and progress assessment. Thirdly, the involvement of university staff in these activities must be regarded by central leadership as worthwhile and acceptable functions of University staff.

Role of NGOs

NGOs have begun to have a significant effect in the development area and this has not been lost on governments in Third World Countries who have, sadly, found many of their own massive development efforts coming to nothing, India has the longest history and the widest experience of NGOs working with the rural poor. The NGOs in India represent an independent, autonomous and vibrant sector which can work on social and developmental problems of the country with a degree of freedom that the government institutions do not have and a sense of commitment and concern. The NGOs in the area of development work at the grassroot level. They look at the issues of development from the viewpoint of the poor they see the acts of development on their communities and try to affect change with people they know and whose problems they share.

In order to move towards the integrated development, NGOs should keep in mind and work towards the following:

1. NGOs' plans, programmes and strategies must be taken up, not just on the needs of the poor, but by the people themselves.
2. The programmes should not only be relief/concern/ actions but that the models) experiments must have a larger influence. Advocacy by NGOs is essential because of few "good" NGOs cannot change the system unless they change other forces in the process.
3. The role of NGOs' lies not only in experimenting and creating models of alternative development but also in action and resistance. At the same time their role must be to provide information, to communicate issues, to change public opinion and to build up support.
4. NGOs' demands must be clear. Those working with the rural poor must therefore pressure for the ownership and control of the primary productive resources by the rural poor including women. Where ownership is not possible, the demand for access and control by the poor is a must.
5. Lastly and most importantly NGOs should not cause regional imbalances either by going into areas where work is already being done or by concentrating too many resources in one area.

So far the NGOs have focused their attention on the delivery of services to the rural poor, but that these efforts would not change the situation in any substantial way unless the root causes of poverty were themselves attacked, for achieving this the following aspects should be taken into consideration.

1. The need and rational for organisations of the rural poor, the different strategies being used by NGOs and

a collective evaluation of the attempts made so far and the efforts that need to be made in the future.

2. The mobilisation of funds and other resources needed for organisations of the rural poor; and the relationship and notion of partnership necessary between "donors" and action groups.
3. The need for consolidation of NGOs' activity and solidarity between NGOs themselves and between NGOs and researchers, professionals and communications.

Now that there is an increasing number of NGOs which recognise the need to organise the rural poor as a prerequisite to tilting the balance of power and resources in favour of the poor, it is necessary that such NGOs make a serious attempt at forming alliances with those working for the same cause. Alliences are also necessary between NGOs using different "entry points" or those developing an expertise in specific areas like education, health, legal aid, credit, research, communication etc. assuming, of course, that the ultimate aim of these NGOs is also to empower the rural poor. The present system of education, research, media and communication, the judiciary, technology and science etc. are all controlled by and serve the dominant classes. These forces can only be proposed by a movement that links up with and uses these a very instruments of oppression. Thus alliances are necessary not only between the minded NGOs but also between these and progressive journalists, researcher, communication experts, scientists, professionals and again at multiple levels participatory and action-oriented research done in close collaboration by activists and researchers in necessary and help both action and theory. Collaboration needs to be improved also between NGOs and groups working on alternative media and communication. With the help of communication experts, NGOs need to establish alternative networks of information, develop alternative communication programmes, document NGO efforts in the region and disseminate this information as widely as possible.

Conclusion

The university is found consciously and constructively to relate its activities to integrated development by being responsible to national and specific community needs. On the other hand the role of NGOs in various fields has been increasingly recognised from pure charity, relief and welfare-oriented approach this sector has in recent times suitably moulded and equipped itself to meet the development needs of the society. But for the achievement of integrated development, collaboration, coordination and cooperation among the NGOs, universities and government is essential in the following aspects.

1. Information exchange
2. Preparation, packaging and dissemination of useful information on to the end-users.
3. Upgrading the performance of change agents.
4. Conducting action research relating to aspects and approaches to rural development.
5. Advisory and consultancy services.
6. Designing and organisation of the courses either on or off campus depending on the needs and requests of the public and NGOs.
7. Involvement of end-users, NGOs, Universities and government in the planning of development projects.

REFERENCES

1. Chrise Durke, NGOs Their Role in Development, *ASPBAE, Journal* Vol. No. 37, July 1986.
2. WHO "The Role of Univeristies in Strategies for Health for All. Resolution WHA 37.31 17th March 1984.
3. Development Dialogue, *A Journal of International Development Cooperation* Published by Dag Hammarshkjold-Foundation, Uppsala, 1975, N. 1/2.
4. Venkat Ravi, R., Narayana Reddy, V., Venkataramana, M. (2004), *Empowerment of People*, Kanishka Publishers, Distributors, New Delhi.

20

Integrated Approach of NGOs and Universities towards Community Development

A Perspective

B. S. Vasudeva Rao
Syam Atluri
G. Viswanandha Gupta

The University is a community which serves the people and helps to monitor their behaviour for an action. In fact, the university caters to the needs of the people from time to time. Another assumption is that the community can be viewed as a total entity and the interests of people in terms of their education, economic, social, cultural and political aspects in its integrity. In fact one cannot view the community or people in pieces and it has to be perceived and understood in its totality only. There is a need indeed to develop a critical and experimental attitude of mind in the younger generation. It is through the institution of NGO or the university can be transformed in to "active, genuine and living community where shared activity and purposeful planning are carefully stimulated". The university should be an instrument of social progress. The community of the university has to fulfill the needs in different ways. The university has to employ a process to fulfill these needs of the community and also the Non-Government Organisations act as a bridge between the community and the university. Here it is necessary to say that the university has the characteristics of creating awareness among the students and these students in turn would transmit this knowledge in the community and instrumental creating the awareness in the society. This can be viewed as a reward service by the university to the society as a social responsibility. It is in this regard the NGOs can joins hands with the university and community. The Vedas long back exhorted this unique feature of the community. "Human beings all are as head, arms, trunk and legs unto one another". Viewed in a broader perspective the community life "includes but goes beyond local community to encompass religion, work, family and culture, it refers to social bonds characterized by emotional cohesion, depth, continuity and fullness".

The process of the university which involves knowledge and intellectuals and this knowledge is meant for the good of the society. There has been a tremendous change in the society during the past many years. As a result of these changes there has been a change in the process of knowledge also. In this context the university has to play a crucial role in the process of the changing society. To sustain these social changes there has to be a mechanism with the university system. If we consider the examples of the rural universities there has been a clear linkage between the university and the community especially with the economic and social conditions of the people in the villages. A university is a centre of economic and social life and above all an intellectual centre. There has to be an amicable co-operation between the university, community and the village. Rabindra Nath Tagore's Shantiniketan was created out of the seminal idea that the university and for that purpose any eastern university is invariably linked up with the core of the community, more especially the latter's economic life and the village communities. The existence of the university, according to Tagore "Depends upon the success of its industrial activities carried out on cooperative principle, which will unite the teachers and students and villagers of the neighborhood in a living and active bond of necessity". In fact, the university is not only a centre of intellectual life but the centre of economic and social life. The university besides imparities should cooperate with the villagers and the communities round it.

In a democratic country like ours with free and voluntary form of franchise, the educated people must be able to perform their roles in an effective and committed manner. So it is most important thing to literate the people of the country to have a literate society to function in a responsible way. The Indian constitution also provides equal opportunities, social justice, economic freedom and values of life. We have a political system which acts through Panchyat Raj system of serving people and we have a free and fair economy to earn and live and finally the social obligations to be fulfilled over a period of time. There has been a conflict between the traditional values and the modern values leading to serious problems. And it is here that the universities have to play a crucial role in balancing these issues to maintain the balance.

To maintain this social equilibrium, the social structure has to create a network of institutions to achieve the expected goals and to bring about the desirable results. And this new social structure has to go for new goals involving the industrial growth as it was happened in the west during the industrial resolution. While transforming to the new social structure one should not totally ignore the previous social structure. And as a consequence it should not lead to the corruption in the social system which may lead to serious anti-social consequences. This may lead to a serious crisis in the National character. So ultimately to maintain the balance in the social structure it is essential to have recognized and properly organized institutions to fulfill the goals of the people and the society. It is exactly here that the role of the NGO comes into the picture to play a role to serve the people in the better way. These institutions can continue the spirit of the students to serve the community after the training in the university. And an NGO has a scope to serve and also an NGO can develop its own mechanism to train the students.

The important other factor is that there are many differences in the society on the basis of caste, religion and the languages. Here also the NGOs can play an useful role to contemplate solutions for these differences. The NGOs are the instruments to create an understanding among different categories of people through constant rapport and can create an amicable atmosphere in the community as well as in the society. If the NGO can serve the people in the area of their jurisdiction, these problems can be solved to a greater extent. For the people who are working and people who are supervising the activities the university can contribute in terms of training the people and the NGO can expose them to different work situations. The approach of the government to go for the community development in the rural, urban and tribal areas is a remarkable phenomenon. Under these programmes an overall development of the areas such as education, agriculture, industry, public health are implemented. And the NGO can play important role in these areas and in the programmes of literacy and related programmes the students can play an active role with the help and guidance of the NGO. Then people would be ready to accept the programmes positively and also people are motivated. At this point, the NGOs must take extreme care to be realistic in their approach.

The NGOs can create the necessary opportunities to make an interaction possible between the community and the university. The NGO can be an excellent instrument to bring the university closer to the people. At the same time the people will have a number of opportunities to be exposed and to learn. And for the students the NGO can inculcate the necessary social consciousness. The students after leaving the university may have to face the problem of unemployment which leads to serious frustration. The involvement of the students in the activities of the community could teach them, how to live in the society even without a job in government. In fact the NGOs working in the villages can be the real motivators to involve the youth in the service of the people and the community in the villages.

The intelligence and the abilities of the youth today is misused in various undesirable activities. The NGOs can train the students to involve themselves in the activities of village development which ultimately results in the development of the country. There may be some apprehensions with regard to the role of the NGOs in bringing the universities close to the community. But still it is necessary to involve the NGOs in the process of development of the community and the people in collaboration with the university. The students trained in the universities are not exposed to the problems of people in the villages. For many years this problem was not attended by the rulers and administrators. But today the popular and democratic governments are trying to involve the youth in the service of the people in the villages. And it is at this juncture that there is an urgent need to involve the NGOs in the construction and development of the people, the community and the society. During the British period, the students are involved themselves in the activities to overthrow the foreign rule in a different way. Historically, our society does not have any tradition of students' participation in the community affairs. Rather the students got educational training for away from the habitation areas to the far-flung places largely in the forests. They were virtually cut off from the stream of society's life. This is what we learn about our ancient educational Gurukula system. Even during the Muslim period, the students remained indifferent to the problems of the community. Now the things are totally different, there is an urgent need for construction and development and NGO offers one of the logical alternatives.

REFERENCES

1. Lumsden K.G. (1974) "*Efficiency in Universities: The La Paz Papers*" Elsevier Scientific Publishing Company, New York.
2. Piyasoma Medis (1986) "Methods and Techniques in Rural Communication" *Adult Education and Development*, German Adult Education Association, Vol. 27 October.
3. Subba Rao. D (1981) "University and Extenstion", *Researcher, Journal of the Research Scholars' Association*, Andhra University, Visakhapatnam.
4. Sumati Dubey and Ratna Murdia (1983) "*Organizational Designs and Management Methods for Human Service Organizations*", Himalaya Publishing House, Bombay.
5. Vasudeva Rao B.S. (2004) "*Evaluation Studies*" Published by The Associated Publishers, Ambala Cant, New Delhi.

21

A Policy Dialogue between Universities, NGOs and Corporate Sector for Social Development

S. Vijaya Kumar

Background

The new millennium has opened a hopeful development opportunities to the world. As quoted by Jeffrey Sachs, countries has marveled at the dizzying progress of the new internet age, the new global interconnectivity, and the seemingly endless flow of new products, new ways of linking people and production system around the world.

In addition, at the historic September 2000 UN meeting, the world leaders convincingly expressed a global determination to end some of the most challenging problems inherited from the twentieth century. They conveyed the hope that extreme poverty, disease and environmental degradation could be alleviated with the wealth, the new technologies, and the global awareness with which we had entered the twenty-first century. They came out with a Millennium Declaration, which can be achieved through social partnership between various stakeholders. At macro level such stakeholders are non other than Human Resource at Universities, Development Professionals at National and International NGOs and the potential donors of Corporate Sector.

The time-bound and quantified Millennium Development goals of the declaration are:

Goal 1. Eradicate extreme poverty and hunger. Halving the proportion of people living on less than a dollar a day and halving malnutrition.

Goal 2. Achieve universal primary education. Ensuring that all children are able to complete primary education.

Goal 3. Promote gender equality and empowerment. Eliminating gender disparity in primary and secondary schooling, preferably by 2005 and not later than 2015.

Goal 4. Reduce child mortality. Cutting the under-five death rate by two-thirds.

Goal 5. Improve maternal health. Reducing the maternal mortality rate by three-quarters.

Goal 6. Combat HIV/AIDS, malaria and other diseases. Halting and beginning to reverse HIV/AIDS and other diseases.

Goal 7. Ensure environmental sustainability. Cutting by half the proportion of people without sustainable access to safe drinking water and sanitation.

Goal 8. Develop a global partnership for development. Reforming aid and trade with special treatment for the poorest countries.

All these goals need to be achieved by 2015.

While reviewing the progress made across the countries Mr. Kofi Annan the Secretary General of United States say:

> "We will have time to reach the Millennium Development goals world wide and in the most, or even all individual countries. But only is the break with business as usual. We cannot win overnight. Success will require sustained action across the entire decade between now and the deadline. It takes time to train the teachers, nurses and engineers; to build the roads, schools and hospitals; to grow the small and large businessable to create the jobs and income needed. So we must start now. And we must more than double global development assistance over the next few years. Nothing less will help to achieve the goals".

The statement clearly highlights the importance of new stakeholder partnership in development. Countries in isolation cannot achieve the target. Countries need to go beyond the financial investments to achieve the goals, need to design new strategies, need to involve different human capabilities, invest innovate skills and utilize the appropriate technologies. Such national level strategies would dramatically enhance chances of success.

Where India Stands

Let us examine where we stand in relation to the Millennium Development goals.[1] In other words assess the achievements made so far with regard to the eight indicators specified in the MD Goals.

Goals and targets from the Millennium Declaration	Indicators for measuring progress	Value of indicators in 2005 or closest year
1	2	3
1. Eradicate extreme poverty and hunger	Population below poverty line	34.7%
	Underweight children	47%
2. Achieve universal primary education	Children aged 5-9 years attending school	87%
	Pupils starting grade 1 who reach grade 7	84%
	Literacy rate of 15 to 24 years olds	76.4%
3. Promote Gender Equality and empower women	Women in wage employment in the non-agricultural sector	42.5%
	Ratio of literate females to males among 15 to 24 years old	0.68
4. Reduce child mortality	U 5 mortality rate (per 1000 live births)	22
	Infant mortality rate (per 1000 live births)	63
5. Improve maternal health	Maternal mortality ratio (per 100,000 live births)	550
	Births attended by skilled health personnel	43%

(Contd...)

1	2	3
6. Combat HIV/AIDS, malaria and other diseases	Contraceptive prevalence rate	59
	Prevalence rates associated with Tuberculosis per 100,000	287
7. Ensure environmental sustainability	Population with access to safe water	86%
	Population with access to latrine/toilet facility	30%

No doubt India has made significant gains in human development over the past decade. But still the country faces a number of challenges to meet its target of improving the well-being of all citizens and thereby achieving the MDG. Lack of education limits access to off-farm jobs. Still, many children do not complete a five-year primary education program, especially girls and children from scheduled castes and scheduled tribes, some because they never enroll but particularly because many drop out of school. Ill health is a particular concern for women and children. Improving delivery of basic health services is essential. Still a non-negligible proportion of the population lives in unhealthy conditions, lacking access to safe water and sanitation.

The Missing Link

The above information clearly indicates the mixed results of achievements and remaining the future challenges. We are at the edge of 2005 and we have hardly a decade of time to reach the UN declaration targets. Here the fundamental question is—Can we achieve the specified results within the specified time frame? Whether the existing policy facilitates the required strengths at different sectoral level? Do we have sufficient knowledge base and technology to achieve the goals? Such fundamental questions may need to be examined because many of such commitments of the past century were not achieved by India. For instance, health for all by the year 2000 (committed in 1978) and universal access to primary education by the year 2000 (committed in 1990)—in both these commitments India is lagging much behind compared to few developing countries. The reasons for such results analyzed by the researchers and academicians are basically the missing link between the academicians/researchers and the policy designers. In addition, financial limitations and operational (top to bottom approach) and administrative constraints in the sectoral departments affected the progress of the programs.

What is Next Strategy?

There are many challenges however there are opportunities to meet these challenges. It is essential to have coordinated efforts across various sectors—Government departments, Non-Governmental Organizations, Corporate Sector, Universities, Research Organizations, Civil Society Organizations and National and International Donors. Such coordinated efforts required a strong multi-sectoral institutional mechanism that will ensure and enable MDG to happen. It is also essential to seize the opportunities, harness the best practices that could be replicated. More importantly it is essential to provide a unique academic base for garnering the science-based, cross-disciplinary understanding needed to confront the practical changes of the intended development.[2] In fact, the progress of the Millennium Development Goals rests on thorough scientific understanding of the underlying challenges of specified. As mentioned earlier the social partnership between different profesionalized expertises is the best solution. Particularly the social partnership between Universities, Non-Governmental Organizations, and Corporate Sector is the suggested model through which a scientific approach to achieve the MDG can be designed. Because each one of these institutions are having different focused strengths, which can be brought under one umbrella to reach the destination.

Social Partnership

The social partnership can be established through a policy dialogue. Strong inter exchange tripartite network need to be designed between the partners—Universities, Non-Governmental Organizations and Corporate Sector. Looking into the fundamental vision of these institutions indicates that universities basic vision is to produce skilled professionals, innovate new technology and help the policy makers with practical solutions. Similarly non-governmental organizations are strong enough to reach the grassroots. Corporate sector is now entered into a new dialogue called "corporate social responsibility" through which different community development programs are supported.

Analyzing the social partnership between these three institutions, Corporate Sector is working with non-governmental organizations is a recent phenomena. Whereas, with few exemptions and limitations, no such development partnership has been working between universities and non-governmental institutions. However, there is much scope to establish such tripartite partnership for development. Such social partnership can be designed by strengthening the weakness of each other institutions. Each one of these three institutions can create atmosphere to seize the opportunities to work together. In this process let us assess the strengths, weakness and opportunities on which each one of these institutions can have a policy partnership dialogue.

Strengths

Universities	NGOs	Corporate Sector
• Multi-Cluster Disciplines	Grassroot professionalism	Corporate Social Responsibility
• Fundamental Research	Working with people	Funds
• Science and Technology	Networking & Coalition	Strong Network
• Human Resource	Action Research	Research & Development
	Action Learning	Important role in Public Policy
	Employment	Agents of Development
	Influence Public Policy	Technical Know-how
	Agents of Change and Development	

Weakness

Universities	NGOs	Corporate Sector
• Translating Research into Development • Network • Suitable Human Resource with development focus • Coalition Research • Communication • Advocacy • Theoretical learning • Application of Fundamental research	Functional Research Skilled staff Translating research output into action	Reaching grassroots

Opportunities!

Universities	NGOs	Corporate Sector
• Networking with NGOs and Corporate Sector	Networking with Universities	Network with universities
• Sharing and Learning	Information sharing universities	Drawing HR from
• Involve in Action Research universities	Drawing HR from scholars	Training the
• Professionalized Human Resource Development	Training the scholars	
• Coalition programs	Relearn	
• Cross-Functional research and learning		
• Can change from Fundamental/Theoretical Research into Functional Research andApplied research		

The above analysis on strength, weakness and opportunity indicates that all the three institutions are having certain strengths of their profession, which can be shared and at the same time certain weakness, which can be overcome through policy dialogue (opportunities for partnership).

How to Establish Social Partnership?

Basically universities are built on multiple clusters—social sciences, biological sciences, earth sciences, health sciences, environmental engineering and agricultural sciences. By joining these disciplines under one roof, the universities can better connect the required science and technology with public policy to find practical solutions to challenges under MDG. Similarly with such knowledge base and human resource universities can provide technical as well as human resource support to the non-governmental organizations. Through partnership dialogue opportunity can be created to design "young professionals" program with the help of corporate sector.[3] This will help (both monitory and knowledge) the students of different disciplines to enhance their knowledge on social development. As a project work, for a brief period, final year students can also be encouraged to work with non-governmental organizations. Most of the research taken up by the universities is mainly focused on theoretical concepts. Now it is time to diversify the research from theoretical to functional. It is also essential to conduct multi-cluster and multi-disciplinary research studies. Any research topic should have application component. Applied research will only help the non-governmental organizations in designing the appropriate action programs. In this way universities can expand their scope and limitations under the research activities.

Similarly non-governmental organizations can provide global practices/information, particularly on how to reach grassroots, how to implement action programs and what are the development trends, to the universities so that the students/scholars can review and refresh their knowledge on social development. Non-governmental organizations are very strong in action learning and are the agents of change. However, the past experiences shows that some times they may fail to translate the research outputs into action outcomes. Such weakness can be overcome by appointing skilled scholars from the universities. In addition, scholars can be encouraged by the non-governmental organizations to design action programs based on their theoretical experiences.[4] In coalition, non-governmental organizations (vice-versa) can organize TOT[5] programs to the students of various disciplines. Coalition research, information sharing through newsletters are some of the initiatives that can be thought of by the non-governmental organizations as well as by the universities. In this process, with its structured scope and limitation, Corporate Sector can play a strong and meaningful role of providing financial supporter to the intended development programs. Most of the Corporate Sector is now working towards SA 8000, OHSAS 18001, and OIS 14001.[6] To achieve such international standard certificates Corporate Sector is spending amount on social development activities.[7] In this particular program, universities can have a dialogue with the corporate sector to have scholar exchange programs to share the technical knowledge. In this way each one of these three institutions can explore network relationships. If such partnerships are developed definitely India will achieve the targets specified under Millennium Development Goals. Collective approaches collaborated responsibilities always result in success. Otherwise achieving MDG by 2015 will be one more "political slogan", which can be tagged to our history of development.

To Conclude

With little modifications let me bring the comparative concept brought by Jeffrey between clinical medicine and development economics to end the poverty in our lifetime by achieving the MDG.

There are five main lessons of clinical medicine relevant to clinical social development. Lesson one is that the human body is a complex system. Lesson two is that complexity requires a differential diagnosis. Lesson three is that all medicine is family medicine. Lesson four is that monitoring and evaluation are essential and Lesson five is that medicine is a profession. These five key lessons of clinical medicine have clear counterparts in good social development practice. First development is a complex system that needs clear and in-depth understanding about the structure of the system. Second, development professional, like medical clinicians, need to learn the art of differential issue based diagnosis. Third social development, like clinical medicine should view treatment in "family" terms, not just individual terms. Fourth good development practice requires monitoring and evaluation, and especially a rigorous comparison of goals and outcomes. And finally the development community needs to strengthen itself in ethical and professional standards. Now social development needs to replace the past twenty years of development practices, known for individual approaches. A clinical social development approach will point the way to a better strategy and create opportunity to achieve Millennium Development Goals by 2015.

REFERENCES

1. See, UNDP Human Development Report 2005, New Delhi: Oxford.
2. See, Jeffery Sachs (2005) "The End of Poverty: How we can make it happen in our lifetime" London: Penguin Books.
3. CAPART is having young Professional program. Under this program once in a year CARPET selects the young students/scholars from different universities to work in their regional centres. During thistTwo years program the selected young scholar will be supported with suitable remuneration. In fact this is appreciated opportunity to the selected students/scholars to learn about the ongoing development programs, grassroot scenario and how to design action program. The universities with a policy dialogue with corporate sector can work out such opportunities.
4. Centre for Alternative Development Strategies, South Africa through its journalistic program encouraging scholars from different African universities to come up with concrete action plans and recommendations to help the development in Africa.
5. TOT = Training of Trainers.
6. These are the international certificates awarded to the corporate sector who have achieved the basic standards under corporate social responsibility. In this Process there is lot of scope for them to support the non-governmental organisations to taken up community development programs at grassroot level. SA 8000 (Social Accountability International); OHSAS 18001 (Occupational Health and Safety Management System) OIS 14001 (Environmental Management System).
7. For instance, Reddy foundation for Human and Social Development, Krebs Bio-chemicals Limited, Byrraju Foundation from Andhra Pradesh, ITC and ILRD of Calcutta, AMUL, ESCORTS and so on are working for social development.

22

Community Development

Role of Universities and NGOs

A. Janitha Begum
G. Lokanadha Reddy

Universities have a significant role in supporting knowledge driven economic growth strategies and in the construction of democratic and socially cohesive societies. Higher education is more than the capstone of the traditional educational pyramid. It is a critical pillar of human development world over. In today's lifelong learning framework, higher education provides not only the high skills necessary for every labour market, but also the learning and training essential for teachers, doctors, nurses, engineers, civil servants, humanists, artists, entrepreneurs, scientists, social scientists and several such personnel. Since Independence there is a vast growth of universities in India producing good manpower and technical expertise from basic pure sciences to applied sciences, social and behavioural sciences. As a result, the country is experiencing very good trained manpower facilities in different fields. This trained manpower must be in functional use to disseminate the knowledge created and skills developed at University level for shaping the public attitude towards development oriented works by the government.

NGOs normally involved in literacy and non-formal education programmes, development of vocational and technical training, technology transfer, small enterprise development schemes and so on. The NGOs are funded by the State and

Central Governments apart from charities. In other sense, they are the link between the Government and the people for promoting developmental projects and welfare schemes in the society/community. Despite the attempts of the Government, education and training have not been accessible for many in the informal sector. Apart from problems of location, disruption of regular worklife and other similar difficulties, formal education and training are not easy to access.

Unless there is a direct linkage between the educational institutions and NGOs the knowledge, skills and competence generated, infrastructure development, appropriate programmes of education may not reach the needy people. Due to a high level of expertise combined with insight, empathy and flexibility of approach, many times NGOs are more successful than the Government bodies in the promotion of Education and Training in the informal sector. The Government has been honest enough to acknowledge the importance of involving NGOs in the various developmental tasks of the country. In the first Five Year Plan itself it was noted that NGOs would have to bear the major responsibility for organizing various activities in different fields of human welfare and development. Over the years, this recognition has increased in scope and emphasis. The Seventh Plan explicitly expressed the intention to involve NGOs in the implementation of developmental programmes, particularly in the rural areas. The period since India's independence witnessed a dramatic increase in the numbers of voluntary organizations. Between 1953 and 1980 the number of NGOs increased five-fold from about 1800 to more than 8000.

Linkages between Universities and NGOs

The Universities and NGOs should go hand in hand to strengthen the efforts of the Government in accelerating the community/rural development programmes in the form of developing scientific attitude, appropriate skills in the people. The Universities and NGOs can work together in promoting, teaching and training, research and extension and nation-building and cohension activities for integrated development of the community.

Teaching and Training

Universities play a vital role in providing the high skills necessary for every labour market by providing teaching and training to teachers, doctors, engineers, civil servants, humanists, entrepreneurs, scientists, etc. By training and teaching to such personnel one can develop the capacity and analytical skills that drive local economies, who support civil society, who teach children, who lead effective governments and who make important decisions which all affect the entire society. Higher education assists the growth and improvement of the institutional regime through the training of competent and responsible professionals needed for the overall development of the society.

In this aspect NGOs can develop links with the Universities in the following lines.

— NGOs can identify the need-based courses and suggest the same at University level. They can orient themselves in informing the expectations of the employees to the public, as there is imbalance between demand and supply of Education or manpower.

— As the NGOs of our country are capable of reaching the deprived masses or disadvantaged groups, they can easily identify the employment opportunities, so that both the students and the society can be mutually benefited.

— Training in Technical and Vocational skills alone is insufficient. It must be combined with basic business. This aspect can be effectively taken by the NGOs.

— Marketing and entrepreneur skills are very essential in the world of Globalisation and Privatisation. NGOs have the potentiality to provide these opportunities to the fresh graduates who come out of the Universities or even the courses are going on.

— Theory oriented courses are run by the universities. NGOs can provide technical support to the theory oriented courses offered in the Higher Educational Institutions. In other sense, by virtue of direct link with the public they should persuade the universities about the type of practical knowledge the students require to deal with the field conditions. And such practical components/experiences must be well integrated with the theoretical aspects of the academic programmes from even school level to University level. In each course, the curriculum must reflect the local-state and global needs of the society, thereby the students will be the fittest survivors and service providers in the Job market.

— NGOs can create awareness in the policy-makers regarding market opportunities, expectations of the employers, need based courses etc through seminars and workshops.

— Due to non-availability of the resources most of the postgraduate students could not undertake research activities. NGOs can identify those students and make them to carry out research work by providing them necessary help and resources.

— Only a handful of Postgraduates took part in the extra curricular activities, sports etc. The talents of many remain unnoticed or suppressed. NGO's can provide more opportunities for extra curricular activities and even provide more opportunities to participate in the National and International level programmes/ competitions.

Research and Extension

Universities are the main locus of both basic and applied research. Researches already proved that where the countries share its higher amount for research and development activities in the educational sector have achieved higher productivity. In order to successfully fulfill the educational, research and informational functions in today's world, universities need to be able to respond effectively to the changing needs in education and training and adopt more flexible modes of organization and operation.

— NGOs can identify the socially relevant research projects and they can provide the necessary data to carryout the research activities.

— NGOs can also undertake university supported projects.

— NGOs can specifically cater to the needs of the special population like disabled, differently abled, minorities, disabled due to socio-economic cultural deprivations, natural and manmade calamities. These organizations with the help of university manpower can take up Block level, District level surveys to identify the specific target population and provide the data to the universities for development of need-based research projects. They in turn use the university expertise to assist these special population for organization of educational, social, cultural and income generating activities that stimulate the environment for effective integration of this population with the normal society. Most of the research findings are useful to the community and the same can be disseminated through the NGOs.

— The NGOs can help the Universities in the extension activities such as providing higher education, job opportunities, childcare, nutrition, health, human rights, self-employment, environmental degradation, modern technology etc to the women.

— NGOs can perform their functions effectively in informing adults and adolescents regarding health-care, income generating business, small scale industries, anti-social elements, good recreational activities etc. to tap their potentialities for nation-building activities.

— NGOs can assist the Higher Education Institutions to improve the institutional regime through the training of competent and responsible professionals needed for the overall development of the society.

— NGOs can assist the universities to undertake and implement projects like VPP (Village Promotion Programme) and VAP (Village Adoption Programme) etc to promote rural mass.

— The results of the research should be infused into the local economy with the help of NGOs.

— The generation, transmission, storage, retrieval of knowledge all pursued by the universities. But application of the knowledge generated is the question mark. All the knowledge generated by the University should reach the society. NGOs can be the link-roads between the university and society.

Nation-Building and Social Cohesion

Higher education contributes to the promotion of civic behaviour, nation-building and social cohesion through the transmission of democratic values and cultural norms. This supports the formation and strengthening of social capital.

— NGOs can take up the responsibility in shaping Nation Building and Social Cohesion along with the universities. As NGOs are known for their commitment and dedication, this can be fostered through them. For example, making the youngsters aware of their duties and rights.

— NGOs' role in protecting the public from Anti-Social Elements can be done effectively.

— They can ensure the students to equip with core values needed to live as responsible citizens in complex democratic societies. The richness of local cultures and values can be made known to the youngsters and public through NGOs'.

— The social cooperation Higher education institutions can be fostered through the strong networks of the NGOs'.

— In the context of globalization and a borderless market, new forms of competition, exchange of information and communication technologies are needed. NGOs can promote new technology developed by the universities by organizing shows, seminars, workshops etc.

— Universities can bring out changes in the learning and knowledge aspects. It is utmost important that the right values, morals, ethical concerns and patriotic spirit should be instilled in the minds of every educated person. For this, we need specially evolved strategies and training programmes, which can be effectively done by NGOs.

— NGOs can act as bodies for the promotion of human rights, by identifying the violations of human right areas. Today the society is more or less violence driven. Concern with human rights cannot stop with the enunciation alone. There is need for more positive and operational steps. NGOs have taken effective measures in Asia, Africa, Latin America, Tunis, San Jose, Bangkok etc. Now the people can no longer leave their problems to the Government, but depend on NGOs also for collective action.

A Paradigm to Link Universities and NGOs

NGOs have much strength. One notable weakness is their lack of co-ordination. For example, in Columbia NGOs already established a national network, nearly 2000 NGOs have joined in this network. NGOs' network should start from district level, state level and to national level. As far as the university is concerned, all the NGOs coming under the jurisdiction geographical area of the University can register and link with the universities. As far as India is concerned, there are number of departments in each of the university. The functioning of NGOs also can join with a particular department in which they are interested.

In any university whether it is central or state university, one can find departments like Education, Sociology/Social Work, Psychology, Political Science, Geology, Home Science, Bio-Technology, Economics, Commerce and so on. These departments have very good human resource potential for teaching, training, research and dissemination of information to the society. For example, the Education department can involve in literacy and continuing education activities, training of teacher in the emerging areas like education for children with special needs, use of low-cost aids to create effective teaching learning situations both in formal and non-formal education environments, training of teacher in environmental protection, sustainable development and so on. Likewise, the department of Home Science can disseminate information related to nutrient values of locally available foods, nutrition and health for pregnant and lactating mothers, care to be taken during pre- and post-natal periods, mother and child health, nutrition and health for children aged and working population and so on. The department of Economics and Commerce can workout the modalities of effective maintenance of family budget, small savings, small family norm, human rights, self-employment opportunities and so on. Likewise, the departments like Bio-Technology and Chemistry can sensitize the people about the need for development and use of organic farms, conservation of energy and environmental protection, judicial use of drugs, value of medicinal plants and so on. The department of Agriculture and Animal-husbandry can disseminate the scientific knowledge related to poultry, diary, kitchen, gardening, modern methods of agriculture like drip-irrigation, need for cultivation of commercial crops, judicial use of pesticide for preservation of environment and so on. The NGOs can assist themselves by all possible ways and means to that particular department in the areas of training, technical assistance, identification of resources and population in need of help, providing support in collection of data, designing socially relevant and useful projects. They can assist in reaching the deprived population in the society especially women, adolescents, children, disabled and identifying income-generating projects, small-scale industries, enriching entrepreneurship skills, marketing facilities to these population. NGOs can act as link between the public sectors, private sectors, colleges, schools, administrative officers, health programmes/ officials, politicians, local communities, society, so that the entire work carried out by the university can have its fruits to the society from the higher level to the grassroot level. The efforts of educational institutions should not go unnoticed and their work must be utilized for nation-building activities.

Conclusion

A well integrated programme with proper planning, development and implementation by involving the government and non-governmental bodies by utilizing the expertise at higher education institutions naturally leads for achieving the objectives of any programme intended to improve the quality of life of the people. In such an effort, each and every segment of the society will have its own share in planning, development and implementation of the programme, thereby inducing a sense of self-responsibility to achieve the personal and social objectives of the individual and society.

REFERENCES

1. Keith M. Lewin (1995) '*Education and Development the Issues and the Evidence*' Overseas Development Administration:
2. Simon McGrath et al. (1995) *Education and Training for the Informal Sector* Volumes 1-2, Department for International Development.
3. DAE, Government of India (1997) *Learning for Participation : An Approach to Training in Adult Education*, Directorate of Adult Education, Government of India, New Delhi.
4. Towards an Enlightened and Humane Society (1990) Final Report Committee for Review of National Policy on Education, New Delhi.
5. Digurmathy Bhaskara Rao (1996) *Human Rights*, Discovery Publishing House, New Delhi.
6. Venkataiah, N (2001) *Educational Research in Indian Universities*, APH Publishing Corporation, New Delhi.

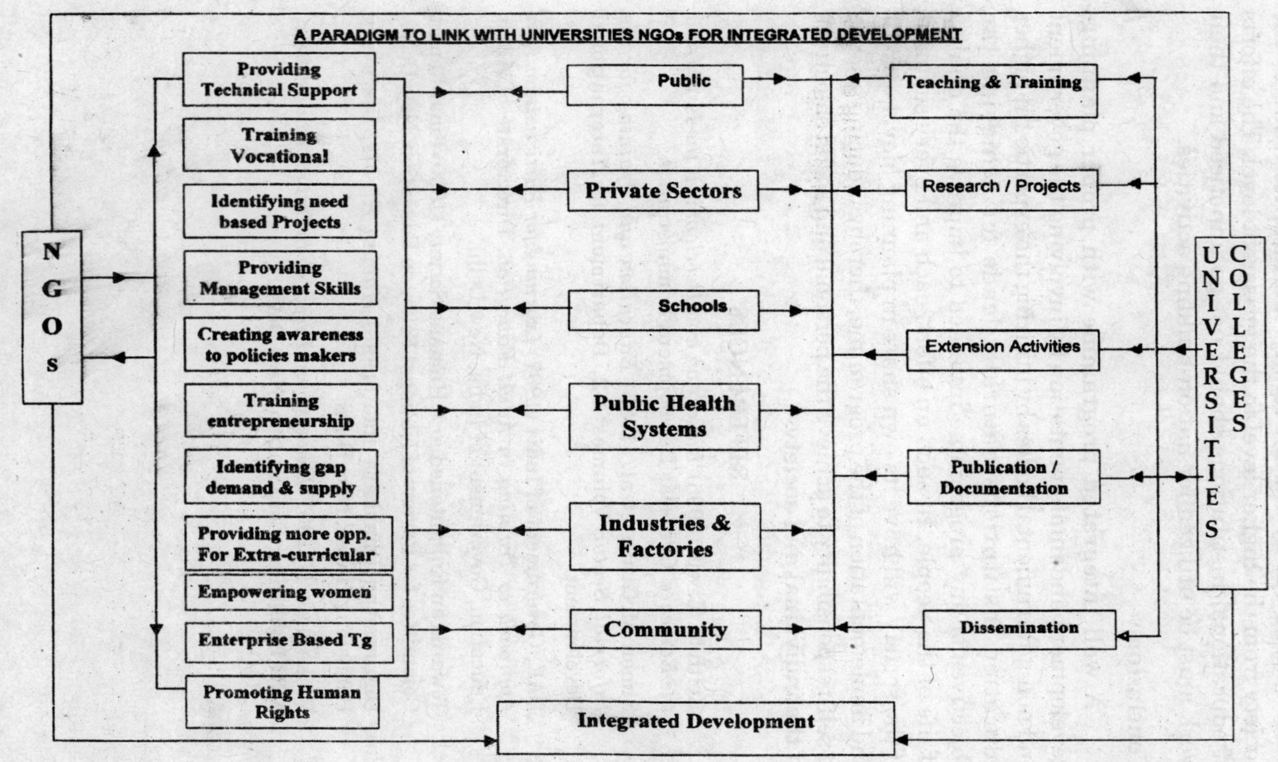
A PARADIGM TO LINK WITH UNIVERSITIES NGOs FOR INTEGRATED DEVELOPMENT
NGOs
Providing Technical Support
Training Vocational
Identifying need based Projects
Providing Management Skills
Creating awareness to policies makers
Training entrepreneurship
Identifying gap demand & supply
Providing more opp. For Extra-curricular
Empowering women
Enterprise Based Tg
Promoting Human Rights
Public
Private Sectors
Schools
Public Health Systems
Industries & Factories
Community
Teaching & Training
Research / Projects
Extension Activities
Publication / Documentation
Dissemination
UNIVERSITIES
COLLEGES
Integrated Development

23

Grassroot Organisations and Universities for Rural Development

Some Viewpoints and Concerns

R. Venkata Ravi
V. Narayana Reddy

Rural Development and Decentralization are interconnected and also much discussed topics in the context of the socio-economic development. The decentralization helps to bring together local initiatives and local knowledge for the development of rural sector. The process of decentralization mainly intended for devolving of functions and authority that give opportunities for the people to play their role, which can ensure initiatives and involvement by the community in the development activities at grassroot level. The basic idea of the decentralization is to enable those, who are influenced by the decisions related to their development as to take part in such decision-making process. In Indian context, constitutionally endowed democratic decentralization through Panchayati Raj Institutions (PRIs) is best suited to operate at and within the community level. Thus it is seen as a vehicle for mobilizing people and resources for the development initiatives at grassroot level. Because, the PRIs enable involvement of the people representatives in the decision-making process related to the planning and implementation of activities for socio-economic development with social justice (Jain, S.P., 2003). The 73rd Constitutional Amendment (CA) has strengthened the PRI by granting the status of local self-government and they are brought to the center stage of the development administration in our country.

At the same time, creation of Community Based Organizations (CBOs) like User Committees and Self- Help Groups (SHGs) have influence on local self-governance, as they exist parallel with the constitutionally established structure of Panchayat Raj Institutions. On the other hand, the Community Based Organizations have become new channel for enlisting people's participation and also to manage the resources and services in the rural areas (Benjamin Powis, 2003). Surfacing of this kind of grassroot organizations has created a new situation in process of decentralization in rural areas. The emergence of these organizations has created scope for horizontal linkages among various organizations and also chance of confrontation cannot be ruled-out with each other in managing the development process in rural areas. The GP as a local self-government, at village level is responsible for planning and implementation of activities for socio-economic development with social justice. To this effect, the GP controls and manages all the resources, services and facilities available in the village such as irrigation water, forest, drinking water, land, organizing the welfare activities, and organizing the people. At the same time, User Groups and other Committees have brought in another phase of decentralization process along with democratic decentralization. Benjamin Powis (2003) terms this process as "second system of decentralization" and the Community Based Organizations (CBOs) are also known as "Stakeholders Association" (SHA). These organizations are mainly for mobilizing and organizing those people whose interest is at stake and also ensuring their participation to work for their betterment by effectively utilizing the available "resources" such as natural, financial, human at the village level. To greater extent these organizations also has the element of democratic flavor both in organizing and managing their activities.

Currently, decentralization policies are being considered as instruments for promoting more social capital formation at the local community level. Thus, promotion of CBO, not only to protect the interest of stakeholders, but also to kindle the local level initiatives based on their needs and capacities. So, the CBO is not just user groups/committees, it is a channel to bring the local community in the path self-reliance and sustainability. The proponents of decentralization and local self-governance have argued for empowerment of local communities and strengthening the capacity of the Community Based Organizations. At the same time, building partnership for horizontal relationship/alliance between local government and CBOs is viable strategy for achieving development in rural areas. Primarily the Panchayats and the Community Based Organizations are working to protect the interest of people at grassroot level and are aiming at a common goal of overall development in rural areas. Besides these organizations, another set of organizations' is also working at grassroot level—they are Voluntary Organizations (VOs) or Non-Governmental Organizations (NGOs). Since, NGOs operate at the grassroot level, as the catalyst of social mobilization and also responsive in bringing changes that are much needed for transformation of rural communities. Thus the NGOs have emerged as a suitable alternative for government in the area of development, based on community initiatives (Joshi, R.P. and Narwani, G.S., 2002). These organizations in India have been playing active role in socio-economic development of the communities at grassroot level. Moreover, over period of last five decades, the NGOs in India has gradually changed/shifted their focus in their operations and have become important stakeholders at the grassroot level in the context of rural development. According to Chopra Ravi (2001), the evolution of NGO roles could be traced from charity in 1960s, to handle welfare and relief activities during 1970s, to initiate development process in 1980s, during 1990s and onwards emerged and also engaged in the Advocacy role.

The NGOs have capacity to understand the local needs, problems and resources. They are also capable of involving local people and getting their contribution to experiment with new approaches, strategies and programmes for sustainable development of rural areas for which large scale expenditure/

investment is not required (Yatish Mishra, 2002). Hence, the NGOs are capable of contributing significantly and influence the local level administration. Social mobilization process has to result in formation of people's organizations, keeping in mind various socio-economic dimensions at the grassroot level: Once people are organized, training and capacity building become necessary with a view to change the culture of dependency to a culture of self-reliance. Institutional strengthening of PRIs is also a crucial strategy at the micro-level, in addition to the promotion of CBOs and their capacity building for sustainable rural development. The NGOs, as part of their development profession, are also involved in organizing community/people into various organizations at grassroot level. The organizations are related to women, farmers, youth and also users of various "Resources and Services" like land water, health, education. The NGOs role in organizing the people is aimed at enabling them to come together and work for effective use of resources and services. The NGOs mobilize internal/ local resources and also bring from outside sources for the welfare and development action at grassroot level.

Current Situation in Partnership

The latest developmental strategy focused on building effective partnerships between NGOs (non-governmental organizations), people's organizations and the local government to work together at grassroot level throws up issues that have a direct bearing on governmental policies, practices and procedures. Moreover, establishing horizontal links between these Village level organizations will be an appropriate framework for Community based initiatives for rural development. Furthermore, it is also necessary for effective mobilization and uses of locally available all resources and sustains the resource based development initiative at grassroot level.

The available literature on the subject is mostly indicating the desired direction and also nature of partnership between these grassroot organizations for rural development. Andhra Pradesh is unique in promoting the user groups and committees in the areas of education, water use, thrift, watershed, and youth employment at village level. The Self-Help Groups (SHGs) are organized not only to inculcate saving but also to mobilize the women and empower them to have interface with a large number of government agencies and PRIs for the sustainable development. At the same time, the Constitution backed PRIs also work at grassroot level for enlisting the people participation in the sustainable rural development. In this context, Bandhyopadhyay and others (2002) have emphasized need for an efficient interface between PRIs and SHG as both these organizations are focusing on "people-centered" development. The user groups and committees are also known as Community Based Organizations (CBOs), are different in many aspects from the Gram Panchayat. Because, the GP is a constitutionally mandated institution that has provision for bringing the people into the system under gender and caste based reservations, whereas the CBOs are not having any such reservations to bring the marginalized to the decision-making forum (Benjamin Powis, 2003). However, the linkages between CBOs and GP can enable "convergence" of various facilities and services at village level as both are aiming at use of the locally available resources for betterment of the people in rural areas. At the same time, chance is also more for dilution of democratic decentralization process with the emerging other grassroot organizations in the villages.

The idea of convergence between PRIs and CBO is anchored on a "collaborative framework" that takes into account of the relative strengths of each other. In this line, based on a study Venugopal and Annamalai (2003) have suggested that the CBOs could function as implementation agencies for the PRIs and also observed that this approach may make "PRI" as without much functional role, but discharging responsibilities as local self-government. The study also advocated for functional convergence by these organizations for comprehensive rural development. It is also possible that the SHG in the form of Vigilance Committee at village level can supervise the execution and monitoring of rural development activities. This kind of experiment is going on currently in some part of the Assam

(Aziz Ahmed, 1999). This practice facilitates involvement of people not only in implementation but also monitoring the same. The system can help PRI to more closely work with the people and also for achieving the transparency in the programme management. The Panchayati Raj system has two hierarchies—one is the elected leader and another is the official. The elected leaders are expected to make decisions and that need to be executed by the officials in the Panchayat Raj system. The system of Panchayat Secretary (PS) introduced in the Andhra Pradesh in 2002. But this system is found in some form or other in Rajasthan, Uttar Pradesh, Madhya Pradesh, Kerala and Gujarat. Vijay Kumar and Sudhakar (2003) in their study on the role of Panchayat Secretary (PS) observed that a new kind of challenge is emerging at the village level. As the PS is responsible for the promotion of SHG and other CBOs in the villages, it provides chance for direct interaction between the GP and CBOs at grassroot level. More so, in Andhra Pradesh, the government has also been promoting the User groups/ committees at grassroot level to manage the various resources/ services. The line departments are responsible for promotion of such user groups for the irrigation, forest, education etc. This situation has lead to multiple organizations at village level working along with GP or/and interfering in the functioning of the GP for rural development.

The differences in functioning and resultant conflict could be sorted at the Gram Panchayat level by involving the CBOs in the process. Because a study (Bhat and Venkata Ravi, 2003) has shown that wherever the CBOs have backed the elected Sarpanch, the functional relationship with the Panchayat Secretary is found to be normal and cooperative, as the leadership has emerged from the community to lead the Gram Panchayat. When the elected leader is from the CBO, the possibility of bringing together CBOs, with GP is more due to same leadership in both organizations. The study revealed that this kind of leadership also pave the way for required level of consultation with CBO in decision-making and in implementation of the programmes. A study conducted by NIRD in Andhra Pradesh, Kerala and Madhya Pradesh shows that by and large absence of convergence between CBOs and the Panchayats. At the same time not found any significant level of conflict between these two sets of grassroot organizations (Venugopal and Annamalai, 2003). But, these community-based organizations are meant, on one hand, for organizing the people as users and on other hand to bring out capacity of the rural leadership for restructuring the channels of power and control the access to resources. In a sense, these organizations from socio-political perspective attempt to play the role of GP in their capacity to control and manage the natural resources at village level.

On convergence of health service delivery at village level, a study in Madhya Pradesh by Durga Prasad and Madhuri (2004) indicates clear linkages amongst stakeholders. Because, from the planning stage, purposive strategy has been evolved to enlist people participation through partnership and networking in health service delivery at village level. Apart from officials, SHGs, PRI and village health committees have been involved as partners in the process. As the health service is significant all the partners work together to jointly manage the system. The experiment of M.S. Swaminathan Research Foundation (MSSRF) in Wynad District, Kerala is a unique. A partnership is built for involving local communities, SHGs, Government officials, Farmers and People's Science Movements to preserve local level healthcare system (Durga Prasad and Madhuri, 2004). This partnership is focused on livelihood and bio-diversity in villages. This pioneering effort is to bring all the stakeholders together to have functional and resource convergence. The partnership is working as the people livelihood is involved and the roles are clearly designated and performed. But, the partnership is not for managing scare resource, more so to establish a resource base at village level.

The recent report on Drought by the Government of India (2004) provides evidences for CBOs involvement in providing and managing the relief. In Orissa, a women group (21 members) in Koraput block with their accumulated fund of Rs. 25,000 as their strengths have taken up the responsibility of managing the Public Distribution System (PDS) and earned a considerable profit from the same. Learning from this experiment, the PDS outlets are operated by the Gram Panchayats are shifted to the SHG in the districts of Kalahandi, Bolangir and Koraput in Orissa. In the case of Rajasthan, the PRIs have been entrusted the responsibility of executing the drought relief activities and made available needed resources. The SHGs have formed the basis for executing these relief activities for which the PRIs have provided required quantum of food grains. Moreover, the SHG have provided loans to its members for purchase of food and fodder to overcome the stress of the drought. In the meantime, the NGOs are involved in a large scale in Rajasthan in the drought relief activities and contributed in the areas of healthcare, drinking water, transportation/supply, cattle camps, fodder depots and also relief works. The PRIs have provided required infrastructure facilities and the NGOs have executed the activities with its network of CBO at grassroot. The NGOs role in development programmes was made a beginning during our 7th plan period. According to Joshi and Narwani (2002) the NGOs role are much found in the development aspects like—watershed, forests, women, children, self-employment, and health sanitation. The PR department through NGOs implements the UNICEF programmes on rural sanitation and safe drinking water. In the states like Andhra Pradesh and Rajasthan, watershed projects are executed by the NGOs.

The Panchayat has constituted the Village Education Committees (VEC), which is responsible for managing the delegated programmes for the development of Education at village level. The community participation has been made possible through VEC in the primary education development programmes initiated in many states. The VEC is made up of representatives from all sections and organizations at grassroot level that include women groups and local NGOs (Manohar Lal, 2003). As the VEC is working with the GP, it is necessary to strengthen their partnership to take advantage of the combined strength and capabilities to manage the educational development in the villages. The crux of the whole emerging phenomenon is that the elected leaders in PRI are concerned about their present position and power, sustain the same even in future, but, the NGO/CBO are focusing on the betterment of people in the rural areas. Another aspect, which needs to be considered, is that functionaries in PRIs, are often replaced or transferred that cause the disturbance in managing the grassroot level development. In the case of NGOs, experienced and skilled functionaries are continued for a long time that has comparative advantage in management of the development. The author has many times observed in the discussions with NGOs, that the relationship between NGOs and PRI is very much influenced by the perceptions on both sides that they are mutually interfering in each other domain. In this line clash and conflict was recently seen in Rajasthan between NGO and villagers of its area verse state department of irrigation (Joshi and Naswani, 2002).

Though the multiple organizations can provide more scope for mobilization of community to respond to their needs in the villages, the domination of elite and power groups may exclude the socially marginalized people to advantage of these grassroot organizations (Eshman and Uphoff, 1984; Benjamin Powis, 2003). It is also possible that these organizations can facilitate emerge of potential leadership in rural communities. Of course, it can result in change of the nature and direction of decentralization of power and access to resources. In this process who wins and who looses due to these organizational power need to be seen in the field. The NGOs are catalyst in social mobilization and can bring people in the new grassroot organizations and in development initiations. These organizations can also be a platform for conflict resolving in the rural community. However, as observed by Manish Tiwary (2003) the NGOs are well suited for motivating and organizing village communities, but limiting factor could the numerical strength of the organizations—both NGOs and the CBOs promoted by them. It is not possible for the NGOs to effectively cover the vast geographical area and dealt with large number of CBOs. In such context both people and Gram Panchayats may treat the NGOs as outsider to that area.

Emerging Situation

The GPs have been mandated to look after overall development of villages by creating and maintaining various resources/services and infrastructure facilities. The GP has both elected leaders and full time officer to take all development activities in the villages. The CBOs have emerged with a purpose of promoting thrift and saving (SHG), manage the natural resource (water, forest) and also services (childcare, health, education) at village level. These CBOs are made up of representatives from a specific section of the village community like—mothers, women, and farmers. Thus a new situation has been created, wherein democratically elected GPs and CBOs have to work at the grassroot level. There is also scope for the horizontal linkages between these organizations at village level for maintaining the functional/service convergence (Benjamin, 2003). The emergence of CBO has open up more scope for people participation in the process of managing the development as they work with available resources both to effectively use and also to preserve the same by renewing, particularly in the case of water and forest resources. But, these parallel organizations working at the grassroot level besides GP has also created scope for local level partnership and also bringing in inter-dependence as they are working for the same goal at the grassroot level.

In the case of NGOs, many of them work in the social sector like mobilization, awareness creation, capacity building, and health services. The NGOs also involved in promotion of SHG and promotion of non-farm activities so that they can take up micro enterprises on a sustainable basis. In this sphere also the NGO and CBO have to work on or use the natural resources (like land, water, forest products) to process/sale their products under micro enterprises. Most of the natural resources in the village fall under three categories of property region—(1) owned and controlled by the government, (2) owned by the private, and (3) owned by the community. In this context, as the natural resources consists of both renewable and non-renewable, the claim over the natural resources and control of same for the utilization has potential for complexity. On event of emerging user groups related to these resources throws up new challenges at grassroot level and redefining the roles of the GP, NGOs and CBOs. Emerging another dimension is connected with the NGO, as many of them are grassroot social activities. Consequently, there are NGOs that resent the emergence of PRIs (particular GP), as the NGOs have to vacate space for these constitutional bodies. Poornima Vyasulu and Vinod Vyasulu (2000) have observed that by and large the PRIs are replacing the NGO, as implementation agencies for government sponsored development programmes. With the devolution of powers and resources, a cleavage is becoming visible in many areas between the NGOs and PRIs. It is a matter of serious concern in the context of interference between these grassroot organizations (Joshi, R.P. and Narwani, G.S., 2002). At the same time, the PRI as local self-government attested to control the NGOs investment in development programmes. The PRIs dictate the term while the NGO is using/working on the common or of the government properties and can also collaborate to effectively use the same resource for the welfare and development of village community. Moreover, the NGO and PRIs can work together in partnership as many NGOs are involved in training the newly elected leaders of PRIs as part of their capacity building programme.

The grassroot level partnership has several implications such as (1) if the government services are not channelised, it is difficult to sustain the interest of the members, (2) as result they may withdraw from the organization, (3) in absence of linkages, develop negative attitude (Yatish Mishra, 2002). So, absence of partnership with the various organizations may lead to the dilution of the CBO and gradually disappear and result in lack of people/community (ownership) participation in development process. Thus, Panchayats, Community Based Organizations and Non-Governmental Organizations have been focusing on the decentralised/local initiatives for the development of rural areas. The origin and status of these grassroot organizations are different for each one, but all these grassroot organizations (PRIs, CBOs, NGOs) are working at cross-purpose and for the development of rural areas. It is required to evolve strategies for working together by focusing on the areas of co-operation, methods/models that help for functional convergence and also identify partnership roles for each organization at grassroot level. Currently with convergence approach in rural development and emergence of user groups/ committees as opened up a scope for partnership among grassroots organization.

Emerging Issues

- No Caste and Gender reservation in CBOs
- Elite domination and power centres
- PRIs are sidelined in development activities by these User Groups
- CBOs are considered as political units rather than community initiatives
- Financial Resources/Autonomy is very much lacking to PRIs
- Functional clarity is inadequate in the Government-PRI Structure
- Inadequate preparedness for taking up micro level planning by PRIs
- Need based linkages and functional coordination between NGOs-PRIs
- CBOs need to be technical wings of PRIs

In the light of the foregone discussion, following observations are made regarding the partnership between Gram Panchayats and Community Based Organizations.

- Community Based Organizations are increasing in number, as it can be large and multiple channels for people's participation in rural areas.
- The CBOs are promoted by the NGOs and also by the government department as user groups/ committees to enable the people participate in the resource management.

- The SHGs are becoming vital CBO in the rural areas.
- The CBOs' involvement in management of resources/ services create a sense of ownership among the people and also increase responsibility.
- These CBOs can be a think tank and play advisory role to the GP in planning and management of rural development programmes.
- Chance is more for horizontal linkage and functional convergence among the CBOs and other village level organizations.
- The conflict cannot be ruled out, as the organizations are different in origin, nature and structure.
- Inter-dependence among the CBOs/GP/NGOs for mutual benefits and also for common interest.

The model for the partnership and linkages can vary according to the ground reality in rural areas. However, a collaborative model to converge the services/functions can be suitable. The Gram Panchayat needs to have a forum at village level consisting of all CBOs working in the village and local NGOs and government officials. The forum can prepare micro level plans for the development and welfare of the rural community. At the same time the CBOs can be implementation agencies in their respective field of interest. However, the NGO need to play a facilitating role and for advocacy. This forum can be as "Village Planning Committees" under leadership of the Gram Panchayat.

Tasks ahead in this connection are involving re-orientation of policies and resultant decisions related to autonomy for PRIs purely depend on the following by any state government. They are like—making a clear decentralization Policy, measures for strengthening the PRIs with more autonomy, Micro level planning and collective action at grassroot level, change of attitude among all stakeholders and political willingness to make such objective decision for longlasting changes in administrative set-up and share in the power and authority along with financial resources.

SUGGESTED MODEL FOR GRASSROOTS PARTNERSHIP—1

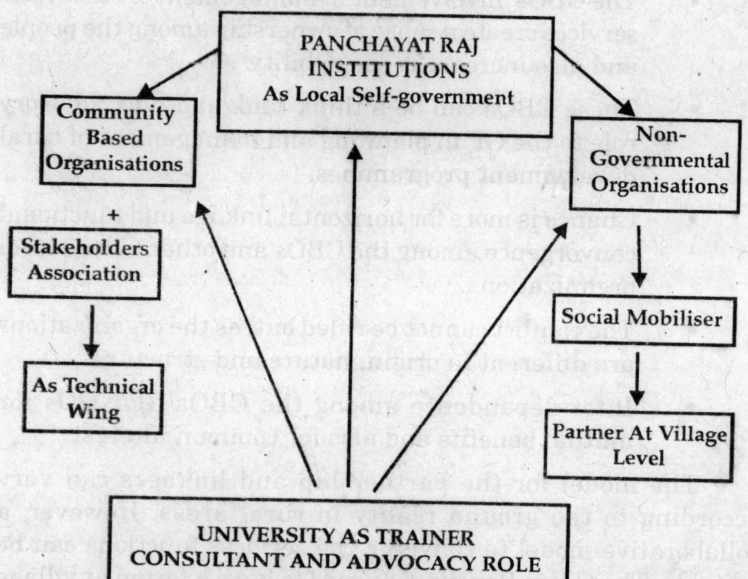

SUGGESTED MODEL FOR GRASSROOTS PARTNERSHIP–2

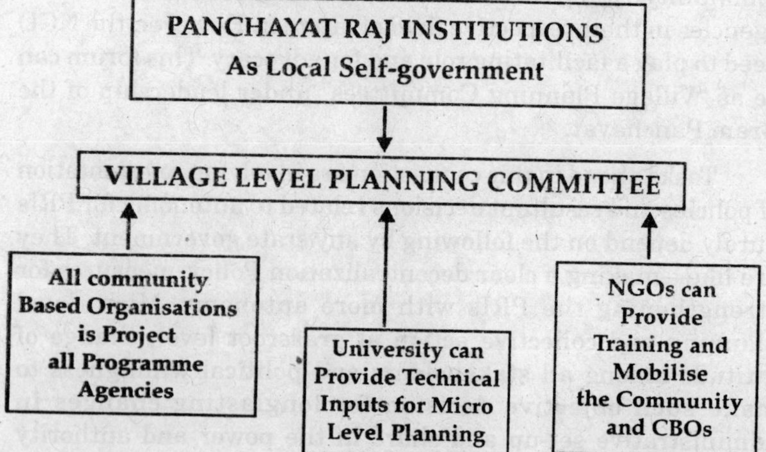

As the situation emerges, wherein all these grassroot organizations—Panchayats, NGOs and People's organizations/ community based organizations are equally important from the part of socio-economic development with social justice in the rural areas. But, it is the need of the hour that NGOs and PRIs have to give up the attitude of working in isolation, superiority complex and treating as competitors. It is very much required that mutually they could contribute in the development process. It is very important to rely on each other's strength to make community based initiatives for the comprehensive development of rural areas.

Common Goal

The Panchayats, NGOs and CBOs are working for the goal of rural development through effective organization and proper management of resources and services at different level. In the future, community initiatives in form of Users Groups and Stakeholders Association would play an important role in the area of decentralized management of development in rural areas. These grassroot organizations need adequate technical and professional support to perform their roles and discharge their responsibilities. In this context the Universities as professional institutes can play significantly to provide required support to the various grassroots organizations. The Universities are Think Tanks with a reservoir of professional expertise and technical knowledge in the various branches of knowledge. This team of faculties could be very useful to guide the organization and people to manage the development.

On the whole the linkages between University-Panchayat-Communities is very much required in the present-day society as the development is mostly "Knowledge Based" and "People-Centered". Moreover, the current trend in the development administration is more focused on decentralisation, wherein scope for different kinds of partnership is also increasing. The University system has been working on the strong three—pillars, namely Teaching, Research and Extension. Within this framework, "Social Capital of all" can be effectively put into use for the overall development of the society. The closely netted linkages are very much necessary so as to share the available knowledge and experience in the affairs of the community in which we are all living.

SUGGESTED MODEL FOR GRASSROOTS PARTNERSHIP–3

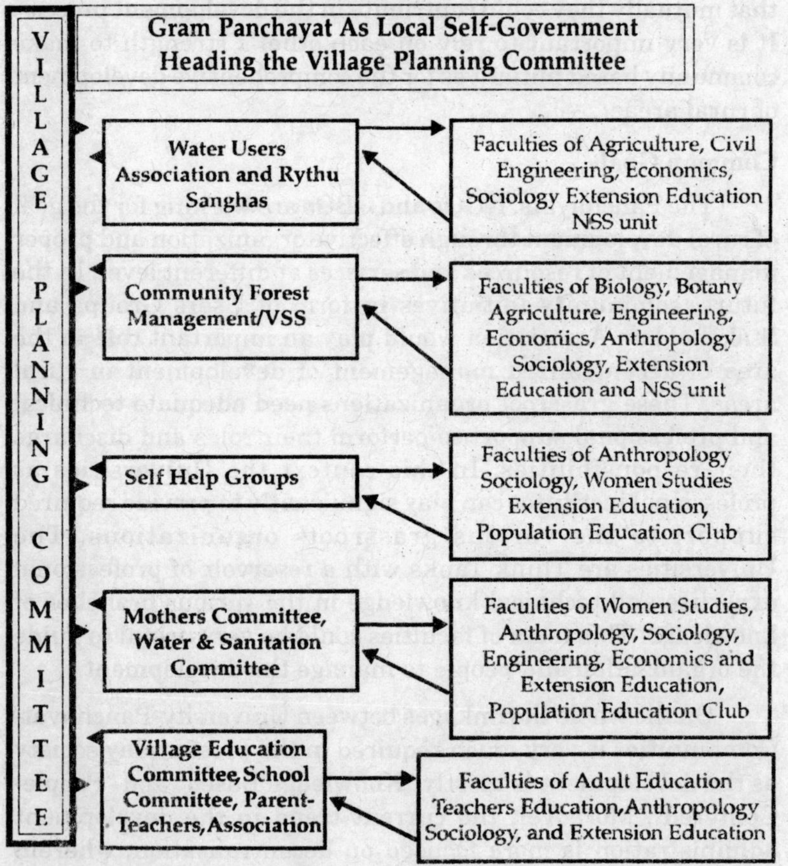

PARTNERSHIP MATRIX

	Panchayats	NGOs	CBOs	University
	1	2	3	4
Primary Role	Local Self-Government work for the development at grassroot level	Development agency work as motivator, trainer and facilitator	Channel for people Participation and contribution	Provide the leading role as Think Tank to direct the development
Prime Responsibility	Providing the basic services for the community	Bringing people together and help the community and Panchayat	Making people to manage affairs of the community on their own	Providing all required technical inputs and know-how
Major Functions	Preparing time-bound Micro Level Plans for the development of the community	Helping the Panchayat and community to work together	Manage various service delivery system and also resources	Analysing the different delivery system operating and develop appropriate system suitable for the community
Problem Identification	Through the participation of all stakeholders	NGOs could play major role in Systematic identification problems	Different Users Groups and Stakeholders Association work for Rapid Assessment of the situation	Can use the Professional skill for this task

(Contd...)

	1	2	3	4
Client Identification	Approving in the selected list of persons and programmes	Facilitator to undertake such process	Service and Resource utilisation status can be known from the CBOs	Can undertake required survey and Research for this purpose
Need Assessment	Consult and bring together all reports	Interface between community (CBOs) Panchayat and University	Providing the information and express the felt needs and common needs	Can provide technical and professional know-how in this purpose
Planning the Action Programme	Primarily planning for delivering basic services	Facilitator role	Providing information and sharing the available local knowledge	Providing the professional skills for planning process
Participatory Implementation	Provide funds and Control the programme	Bring in the external resources to supplement the available resources	Technical Wings of the Panchayat and work as implementation agencies	Process Monitoring and providing project and programme management support
End Evaluation	Commission such evaluation and use the outcome of Evaluations	Information providers	Information providers	Take up Applied Research Project and provide feed back to the Panchayat & NGOs

REFERENCES

1. Moitree Bhattacharya (2002), "*Panchayati Raj in West Bengal: Democratic Decentralization or Democratic Centralization*", Manak Publishers Private Limited, New Delhi.

2. Manoj Rai and Others (2001), "*The State of Panchayats: A Participatory Perspective*", SAMSKRITI, New Delhi, pp. 35-76, 105-130.

3. Aureliano Fernandes (2003), "Aggrandiser Government and Local Governance", *Economic and Political Weekly*, Vol. 38(27), pp. 2873-2879.

4. Shikha Jha (2002), "Strengthening Local Governments: Rural Fiscal Decentralization in India", *Economic and Political Weekly*, Vol. 37 (26), pp. 2611-2623.

5. Bandhyopadhyay D., Yugandhar B.N., and Amitava Mukherjee (2002), "Convergence of Programmes by Empowering SHG and PRIs", *Economic and Political Weekly*, Vol. 37(26), pp. 2556-2561.

6. Pattanaik B.K., (2004) "Community Participation, Panchayati Raj and Rural Health Care", *Kurukshetra*, Vol. 52(3), January, pp. 14-18.

7. Durga Prasad P., and Madhuri N.V., (2004), "Partnership and Networking for Health Development: Initiatives, Successes and Challenges", *Kurukshetra*, Vol. 52(3), January, pp. 4-13.

8. Vijaya Kumar A., and Sudhakar E., (2003), "Role of Panchayat Secretary in Andhra Pradesh—A Study" *Indian Journal of Public Administration*, Vol. XLIX (2), April-June, p. 201-211.

9. Venugopal G., and Annamalai U., (2003), "Relationship Between PRIs and CBOs: Issues of Convergence", *Journal of Rural Development*, Vol. 22(4), pp. 455-486.

10. Vasudeva Rao D., (2003), "Emerging Leadership of Women in Institutions of Local Governance: A Study in Andhra Pradesh", *SOCIAL ACTION*, Vol. 53(2), April-June, pp. 159-168.

11. Vasudeva Rao D., (2001) "Democratic Common Interest Groups Foster Empowerment in Andhra Pradesh", *Social Welfare*, Vol. 47 (11), February, pp. 27-33.

12. Chopra, Ravi (2001) quoted in the "Drought 2002—A Report", Ministry of Agriculture, Government of India, 2004.

13. "Drought 2002 : A Report", Ministry of Agriculture, Government of India, 2004.

14. Joel S.G.R. Bhose (2003), "*NGOs and Rural Development: Theory and Practice*", Concept Publishing Company, New Delhi. 11-100-1005.

15. UNDP Document Community Based Pro-poor Initiatives Programme of Government of India, Sourced from *www.undp.org.in/programme/propoor/apcdppi.htm* <*http://www.undp.org.in/programme/propoor/apcdppi.htm*>

16. "Women's Political Participation and Good Governance: 21st Century Challenges", UNDP 2000, accessed from *http://magnet.undp.org//*

17. Manohar Lal (2003) "Community Participation through Village Education Committee in Primary Education in India" *Journal of Social and Economic Studies* , Vol. XV , December pp. 39-49.

18. Joshi. R. P. and Narwani. G.S (2002), "Panchayat Raj in India: Emerging Trends Across the States" Rawat Publications, New Delhi.

19. Yatish Misra (2002), "*Empowering People: Grassroot Organizations and Rural Development*", Kanishka Publications, New Delhi.

20 Manish Tiwary (2003) "NGOs in Joint Forest Management and Rural development: Case Study in Jharkhand and West Bengal", *Economic and Political Weekly*, December, 27, pp. 5382-5390.

21. Eshman and Uphoff (1984), *Local Organization—local Intermediaries in Rural Development*, Cornell University Press.

22. Perspective on Grassroot Organizations and Rural Development, in D. Vasudeva Rao, S. Vijaya Kumar and R. Venkata Ravi, (Ed) "*Narratives on New Perspectives of Development*", Book Enclave, Jaipur. 2005, pp. 77-90.

Theme V

Dissemination of Development and Welfare Programmes and Research Findings

24

Project on Aids Control among College Students

Kapali

Project of commitment to break the silence not confidentiality. Dr. Peter Piot, Executive Director, UNAIDS at the opening ceremony of the 5th ICAP at Kualalumpur, has emphasized on the significant challenges in AIDS. He has elaborated that in addition to fear and discrimination stigma remains the most significant of matters that need to be dealt with on a war footing, with not only political and academic support, but from the view-point of Human rights. Fighting stigma is not only moral but practical too. This impelling concept made the University of Madras come together with the Voluntary Health Services and its AIDS Wing AP AC to meet the challenges of AIDS, its prevention and control among the most vulnerable sections of growth viz., the student community. A pilot project on AIDS prevention and control among college students direct intervention, supported by the Voluntary Health Services with financial assistance from USAID was conducted for a period of 21 months, from 01.07.1996 to 31.03.1998. With a sanctioned budget of 3 lakhs, the project was inaugurated on September 19, 1996 by the Vice Chancellors of the Madras University and Dr. M.G.R. Medical University, Chennai. The participating colleges were 20, from among those affiliated to the University of Madras and with a student strength of more than 10,000. The Project Director, Dr. N.V.R. Kapali devised a programme on orientation to the principals of these 20 colleges and also the 20 programme officers. Forty student leaders, 2 from each institution, were also imparted pre-service training on 30.10.1996. These student leaders were to comprise the peer group and were given further orientation on counseling by YRG Care at VHS, Chennai under the leadership of Dr. Sunithi Solomon. The project personnel were given training on counseling by the Christian Medical College, Vellore (National referral centre) in October, 1997.

Project Implementation

The 20 colleges identified for the programme were provided with Seed Money to conduct college based AIDS control activities including counseling services to the students.

Feedback

The constant monitoring of the programme yielded the following:

- Need for awareness
- Need for counseling services for students
- Need for identification of High Risk Groups.
- Need for communication strategies.

Support Staff

Apart from the Administrative and Technical personnel, the project officer was on specifically appointed to oversee the activities of this pilot project.

Collaborating Agencies

These included the Tamilnadu State AIDS Control Society (TANSACS), Chennai, Tamilnadu Dr. M.G.R. Medical University, Chennai and Sri Ramachandra Medical College, Deemed University, Chennai. This project revealed many interesting facts, the most significant of which was the spinoff of male and female, crossing the sexual boundary, in coming out openly and demonstrating on condom use and promotion. There was identification of high risk groups for creating overall awareness among students on preventive aspects. Peer counseling made students desire to continue "the mission" and was well targeted.

Rationale

Most of the other projects concerned themselves with direct intervention with vulnerable groups—truckers and commercial sex workers. But the socially cloistered student populations was hitherto considered "untouchable" and "tabooed and secured" and were thought to be above the need of AIDS prevention and control. The pilot project shattered this myth and has indicated that they are also vulnerable to HIV/AIDS infection and the battle against the AIDS epidemic needs go on uninterruptedly by breaking the silence and not the confidentiality. AIDS is an epidemic that does not discriminate. Each and every one of us might be susceptible to its destruction. Hence it is time to realize that the fight against AIDS cannot be left to Government and Non-Governmental Agencies alone. Every individual has the commitment to make life go on defying the AIDS virus. This mission involves the responsibilities that are not just challenging but refined as well. It includes education, caring for others, policy development, fund raising, advising and research. The University of Madras with it hoary heritage of one and half centuries is a storehouse of knowledge and experience. The Department of Adult and Continuing Education has been for the past 3 decades, involving itself in extension and field outreach programmes in various areas that are pertinent for the uplift of society in general and reaching peaks of excellence for the academically inclined. With the view to reaching out to the student community, the Adult and Continuing Education Department have implemented the project on "AIDS control among college students" with the support of VHS, who in turn were given aid by US AID. The programme/project was inaugurated on July 28, 2000, by Hon'ble Arcot N. Veerasamy, Minister for Health, Government of Tamilnadu, in the presence of Dr. N.V.R. Kapali (Project Director). Prof. Dr. S.P. Rajagopalan (Syndicate member) Dr. K. Thiagarajan (Secretary—United Writers Association) and Professor S.P. Thyagarajan, the Dean, Industrial Consultancy and present Vice Chancellor, University of Madras. The University of Madras stepped in for a pioneering role and involved itself in the programme at the right time and in the right direction by initiating rapid action.

Programme Objectives

- To form Red Ribbon Clubs for organising institutional activities at the campus/community level to strengthen the capacity building of the students for developing skills in "Street Theatre" for disseminating messages on reproductive health needs of adolescents.
- To adopt nearby communities for spreading awareness on dreaded diseases such as HIV/AIDS among the members of the public.
- To provide consultancy to students of adolescent needs for maintaining good health.

Strategies

Drawing lessons from the pilot project, the Unives ity of Madras evolved a two pronged attack on AIDS prevention and control among college students. The first line of attack was on the behaviour change and communication strategies for the purposes of delivering direct intervention activities. This was mainly for those institutions which had already been targeted in the pilot studies. The second line of attack was directed towards those colleges which had not been exposed to intervention strategies earlier and which needed to be strengthened in the areas of awareness and counseling.

Duration

This is an ongoing project, which commenced on April 1, 2000. The present report deals with the period from April 1, 2000 to March 31, 2005.

Project Description

The project comprises of the organisers viz., the implementing University, with its Project Director Dr. N.V.R. Kapali and Project Officer Dr.S.Chandrasekaran. The institutions/colleges selected for the programme (10) comprises of the principal, the programme officers and peer educaters as also anyone from the high risk group of youngsters. The programme consists of orientation for the princpals and programme officers and pre-service training and counselling for peer educators. Support was also enlisted from the local NGOs. The orientation for the principal and the programme officer of the colleges helped identify an opinion leader for seggregating 'at Risk' and 'High Risk' target audience for direct intervention.

Implementation

The procedures of implementation were simplified with the following highlights.

- Discussion
- Counselling
- Documentation

Monitoring

In order to effect mid-course corrections, internal monitoring through the Project Director/ Staff and External Monitoring through experts have been done.

Evaluation and Feedback

Exhaustive evaluations were made, based on the feedback received from various agencies.

Follow-up

Follow-up action has been entrusted to local NGOs with the active guidance and supervision of the University Department. Based on the feedback from the pilot project the present programme made the following adjustments.

- The programme was made in consonance with college schedules.
- Counseling needs having been identified through the earlier pilot project, such needs of specifically at risk groups were identified to ensure excellence in counseling.
- Computer internet and e-mail facilities were made use of, to facilitate easy communication.

- Peer educators were given intensive training on various aspects of the disease in order to control, fortify and strengthen them.
- There was rapid rotation of IEC material to facilitate the availability of the same in the various institutions/colleges.
- The project personnel were suitably expanded to ensure prompt discharge of duties.
- The cost escalation was borne in mind while budgeting.

The Project in Brief

The project on AIDS control among college students comprises different kinds of training schedules and innovative actions which ensure its ultimate success. As a run up to the initiation of the project, a Banner campaign under the sponsorship of State Bank of India was initiated. This AIDS control among college student project, fine-tuned its main objectives in order to cover the social side of the issue and for targetting human resources which constitute the elements of success as key factors. In order to get away from the scourge of HIV/AIDS infection, the following had to be kept in mind:

- Timely intervention at the higher education level.
- The urgent need to break the silence on relevant issues and key factors, providing equal access to both men and women in the treatment and care of the disease.
- Taking every required step in the path of prevention.
- Securing the support of the Government/and private sector.
- Bearing in mind the essentials of human rights.
- Accessing and disseminating information.
- Creating a supportive environment for the HIV/AIDS affected.

These parameters have been the culmination of the paradigm shift in population education focus at the international level. As a prelude to the starting of Red Ribbon Clubs in the various Chennai city colleges, an Inter-collegiate competition on 'Men Make A Difference' was held on December 20, 2000 and was presided over by Sister Annamma Philip and the key note address delivered by Dr. N.V.R. Kapali. The Red Ribbon Clubs were inaugurated by Dr. Lakshmi Bai, Project Manager, APAC.

A Cluster level meeting was held on February, 2, 2001 to encourage the partners of the programme to meet and share information and to focus on networking cluster areas. The sharing of information in effect, would avoid duplication of efforts and also promote effective NGOs support. In this connection the APAC/USAIDS funded a Banner on the cluster co-ordinating committee meeting. On 27.04.2001 a Counsellors meet of City NGOs was organised and attended by a representative from APAC and 2 personnel including the project co-ordinator from each NGO which partnered the programme. This meet was organised by Alternative for India Development with Mr. Iruthayanathan, as Project Co-ordinator. The World AIDS Day, December 2001 was observed in grand style with intercollegiate competitions where cash prizes were awarded, pertinent messages delivered by Prof. S.P. Thyagarajan (the present Vice-Chancellor).

Theatre Approach for HIV/AIDS Awareness

While a child knows that the academic tutoring or avunculer advices don't register easily in the memory, adults fully know that speeches or presentations are not the best ways of communicating a message. At present AIDS awareness messages are slowly moving away from the beaten track on to lively performances by Theatre groups. The Indian Theatre group *jagran* "awakening", which was performed at the 5th ICAP is the classic example.

Koothu-P-Patterai/Street Theatre

Alok Roy, Director of *jagran* has said "Body language is easily understood and recognised by all. It cuts across language and national barriers". The Madras University, recognising the potential of Street Theatre, decided to introduce the Koothu-P-Patterai concept in the propagation of the message to control *HIV*/AIDS among college students. Enlisting help from AP AC which was abundantly given by Dr. Sampath Kumar, Assistant Director, NGO-APAC and Mr. Sundar Co-ordinator Koothu-P-Patterai, the Project Director and Project Officer drew up a programme schedule for Koothu-P-Pattarai training. On June 28, 2001 the Koothu-P-Pattarai Programme was inaugurated for College students. The main objectives of the Street Theatre programme are as follows:

- Training to be imparted to 30 peer educators in Koothu-P-Pattarai techniques.
- Peer Educators to form Street Theatre Team in their respective colleges as a sub-group.
- Each team/college to conduct one or two plays each month.

These Koothu-P-Pattarai team were also to perform in other colleges and venues to effectively propagate measures for controlling AIDS among college students. This ploy proved super effective and was much welcomed by the student community. It is heartening to note that these enthusiastic youngsters, on invitation from various NGOs, performed for the public at various venues in many parts of the city such as Trade Fair, Koyambedu Market, Vadapalani Bus Terminus and even the Chennai Central Prison, as also many slum areas. The Koothu-P-Pattarai evolved its own programmes with guidance from the project staff and these programmes mostly comprised of a couple of invigorating songs, meaningful *skits* with relevant messages and excellent *mime* of AIDS related topics. The versatility of the participating youngsters left the audience dumb founded and speechless many a time. There was an occasion when these innovative youngsters beat the traditional *tnoal* instrument called 'Thudumbu' which comprises 16 different varieties of drums which produce crashing but harmonious sounds. Their scintillating performance drew appalause from a 4,000 strong audience at Betram Hall, Loyola

College, Chennai in the august presence of the Hon 'ble Minister for Health, Government of Tamilnadu.

Scientific Meeting

Apart from the Koothu-P-Pattarai, each participating college had to organise one scientific meeting each and every month. These meetings highlighted HIV/AIDS in all its scientific aspects. Through slide shows, video clippings and also lecture demonstration, the science experts such as Doctors or Scientists would chair the session. Sometimes a victim would come forward to share his/her experiences with the dread disease. There were also periodic Debates, Oratorical contests and quiz programmes at intra- and inter-collegiate levels.

Counselling by Peer Educators

The Peer Educators (3 in each college at the start and 6 in each college now) have been assigned counseling sessions. On a one to one basis as also in groups of 3 or more they are required to conduct 12 such sessions each month. However, 12 sessions every month was not feasible because of intervening holidays, examinations and the peer educators' own pre-occupations or illnesses. But it should be acknowledged that in spite of constraints, most of the Peer Educators have achieved their target during the working months of their college.

Mobile Exhibition

Each participant college was required to organise one mobile exhibition during the year with exhibits provided by AP AC. The participant showed such enthusiasm that they took pains to put up the exhibition many times a year in places such as the canteen, lecture hall, library and also at important meetings, attended by VVIPs. There was also a half-day workshop on August 18, 2001 which comprised lecture-cum-Brain storming session. The important aspects under discussion included:

- Female partners of MSM—the risk perspective
- Treatment for female partners of MSM, especially for oral and anal STD

- Programme attended by project/field co-ordinator, field staff and counselors, as also one peer educator from each constituent institution.

Behaviour Surveillance Survey: (BSS Wave 5-9)

The Behaviour Surveillance Survey in a regular feature held every year under the name Wave 1,2 etc. This ongoing programme and its findings have been discussed at regular meetings of the project on AIDS control among students supported by APAC starting from 2001 as BSS Wave-5. These discussions have been held at GRT Grand Days Inn, every year including 2005, where the findings of BSS Waves were discussed. This project helped to understand the strengths among the groups intervened and to guide programme planning and implementation. The participants included Government officials, local NGOs, donors, consultants and partner Agencies. Participants have helped strengthen discussions and have added to the body of knowledge. The State Resource Centre, in co-ordination with UNICEF as participating NGO and the University of Madras put up a stall with exhibition panels and boards supplied by APAC/US AID at the Adolecent Mela conducted by SRC.

This exhibition highlighted the role of the Red Ribbon Clubs in HIV/AIDS prevention and control. There have been regular ESRM meetings for NGOs trained by Koothu-P-Pattarai and other agencies. The meetings were held to share experiences, review performances, identify problems and suggest ways of solving them and to discuss the future plans and sustainability of the program. The pre-entry knowledge of students was assessed to identify basic needs through group sharing experiences of the technical officers of AP AC and their reports. The design of the workshop was identified through discussion of the main objectives which included:

- To explain the communication strategies channel for HIV/AIDS prevention.
- To discuss the importance of condom promotion.
- To state the importance of controlling STD for HIV prevention.

- To demonstrate the use of mobile exhibition.

The methodology used included lecture demonstration, role play, slide show and discussion.

The resource persons were Dr. Bimal Charles, Dr. J Affarullah, Mr. Arvind Kumar and Dr. Sampath Kumar. A post-evaluation was done through a quiz programme and procedural evaluation was done through a questionnaire. Certificates were issued to the participants.

Priorities in the Work Field

The priority included creating awareness among the chosen collegiate population affiliated to the University of Madras. There was identification of high risk groups and capacity-building through counseling, scientific sessions, Street Theatre which included skit presentation, poster preparation, mobile exhibition and training of peer educators. Formation of Red Ribbon Clubs in colleges enables the undertaking of institutional activities at regular intervals for the prevention and control of HIV/AIDS. Care was also given to those students affected by STD etc. The project on AIDS control among college students of the last 5 to 7 years has witnessed a dramatic change in the mind-set of the "young adolescents" leading to severe change in their behaviour, attitude and knowledge of turbulent mind with "unlimited awareness" generated on HIV/AIDS pandemic. The present shift of the virus from the High Risk Population to the General population necessitates the need for working with adolescents who form part of the vast majority of the neglected people who have no access to information and education on the dread virus. The present project with its 11 colleges retained for intervention programme has been implemented with and has been controlled and guided by the Project Officer and the Project Director from the University of Madras. The Red Ribbon Clubs were formed in each college with the principal as patron, the Programme Officer incharge of activities ably assisted by Peer Educators as student leaders and members of the Club.

1. Principal 2. Programme officers 3. Peer Educators

This has brought the entire college under the broad spectrum of programme coverage. The outcome of the project is encouraging and comprises the following:

- Red Ribbon Clubs strengthened
- Peer educator programme implemented
- Knowledge of students on HIV/AIDS increased
- High risk behaviour students identified and subjected to behaviour change processes
- Promotion and usage of condoms
- Awareness created through demonstration of condom usage
- Formation of Theatre sub-groups

Technical approaches included:

- Group sessions
- Street play
- Scientific sessions
- Peer counseling
- Exhibition
- Monitoring
- Advisory meeting for mid-course correction.

Budget

The budget at a glance includes salary for the project officer, postage, telephone communication and stationery charges, travel and conveyance, training expenses, monitoring and evaluation, seed money to colleges, miscellaneous and University overhead charges, leading to a total of Rs. 3 lakhs per year.

Conclusion

Drug use add to the spread of AIDS in the Asian countries and India is no exception. The first objective is to shatter the complacency and bring AIDS to the forefront of the consciousness of every nation, Government and individual. The second is to improve the quality of the regions response and the third is to encourage grassroots actions against the epidemic. This project has been very effective at the local level where some of the best work to reduce stigma is going on and where youth initiatives are most effective. The intervention at collegiate level has sown the seed for awareness and active participation in AIDS control and eradication among college students in the Madras University area. This tempo needs to be sustained in the coming years through implementation of future projects, in order to fully overcome the menace called HIV/AIDS.

25

Development and Welfare Programmes

Role of Universities and NGOs

K.Nachimuthu
G. Lokanadha Reddy

The UGC was set up by the Government of India under an Act (3 of 1956) of parliament in 1956. In 1957, Calcutta, Bombay and Madras Universities came into existence with the faculties of arts, law, medicine, education and engineering. The number of universities increased from 27 in 1950-57 to 295 (Deemed Universities and Institutions of National Importance) in 2001-02. The number of colleges rose from 700 to 12342 during the same period. Enrolment increased from 2.6 lakhs to 60 lakhs (7.5 million students—May 2002 UGC survey). The number of teachers was nearly 4 lakhs. The standards of education and to be defined in the wider sense of the all-sided development of the personality of the individual and his commitment to social objectives and continually rose to suit the changing needs of the country. Students discipline is a cooperative venture in which the teachers, the students, the parents, the press and the educational administrators must join hands and make concerted efforts to create a suitable climate conducive to student growth and welfare. The fact of the society depends upon the caliber of the product of our educational institutions. Education has played a vital role in empowering people socially, politically and economically. This is mote true in knowledge era, when education has occupied centre stage is never before;

today economy of a country is governed by the accomplishments in Science and Technology and capacity it to the people. The University of Calcutta awarded first science doctoral degree in 1911. In 2002, nearly 11,300 scholars were awarded Ph.D degree in the country. (AID survey, 2004) of those nearly 3900 (UGC, 2000) were in science subjects. NGOs perform a very important role in the protection of rights and employment at the local, national and international levels.

In Tamilnadu, there are 21 universities including 12 general universities, five professional universities and four deemed universities. The universities perhaps thought that their main mission was only research and that the job of PG teaching belonged to the affiliated colleges. So that only 25 per cent of PG students are enrolled in the university departments. The Tamilnadu Government has stopped giving grant to any of the new courses of the aided colleges due to the poor standards; the courses have to shift as self financing basis. The following are the list of Universities in Tamilnadu.

1. Alagappa University
2. Anna University
3. Annamalai University
4. Bharathidasan University
5. Bharathiyar University
6. Gandhigram University
7. Madurai Kamaraj University
8. Manonmaniam Sundaranar University
9. Mother Terasa University
10. Periyar University
11. Thiruvalluvar University
12. University of Madras
13. Tamilnadu Dr. MGR Medical University
14. Tamilnadu Agricultural University
15. Tamilnadu Veterinary and Animal Science University
16. Indian Institute of Technology, Madras

17. Tamilnadu Dr.Ambedkar Law University
18. Madras Medical College
19. Avinashilingam Institute for Home Science & Hr. Edn for Women
20. Tamilnadu State Council for Higher Education
21. Dakshina Bharat Hindi Prachar Sabha.

Source: aiu survey, 2004-05.

Some of the administrative function of the University is to administer and release funds, if any, received from National and International funding agencies and to identify and administer innovative programmes for sustainable growth through self-generated funds from consultancy services to industries. NGOs concerned with vocational training—which are out principal concern—are a highly diverse group. NGOs differ from Government agencies in that they have a much cleared focus on the informal sector. They also have a much more explicit link with community development strategies. Therefore, from both the NGO and the University education schemes are often the very groups of entrepreneurial self-employed who have considerable potential for job creation, technology development, and eventually, training provision. This group is too successful for the NGOs, and too unconnected with State structures to get access to the formal sector workshops of the government Centres. This is the very group that the policy community hope will some day graduate from the informal sector to the formal. Not a great deal is currently known about how they acquire their skills. The objective of this study is to examine local and national interventions and initiatives in Tamilnadu relevant to orientation and reorientation of education and training toward self-employment and income generations in one regular school setting. Data have been collected from secondary literature sources, personal interviews and observations and case studies of select interventions. This study is intended to derive lessons about how education and training can be geared to promote self-employment and income generation in the informal sector of the economy. One of the NGO namely, the "Centre for Research in Social Sciences, Technology and Culture (CRSTC)", a unit of GRD Trust in (Coimbatore district) Tamilnadu which bears the name of Public Charitable Trust and is affiliated by Bharathiyar University, Coimbatore.

The Projects completed under this Trust is:

No.	Title of the Project	Year	Participants
1	2	3	4
1.	Science and Technology inputs for the Development of Tribal Women	1994	Tribals of Perianaicken Palayam block of Coimbatore Districts in T.N.
2.	Training Refrigeration Mechanism, Two wheeler mechanism and Food Processing (MEGSAT)	1996	300 Men and Women in Scheduled Castes
3.	Training in Motor Rewinding, Domestic Wiring, Household Electrical Repairing, Hand pump Repairing	1995	Multipurpose of Mechanism Programme
4.	Training in SC Man and Women in Two Wheeler mechanism, Garment making	1995	SC Men and Women (SCP programmes)
5.	Integrated development of the Irula Tribes	1995	Mettupalayam Resource Forest Areas of Coimbatore district
6.	Rehabilitation of the Younger generation of Scavangers	1997	60 scavangers in Coimbatore district
7.	Socio-economic development of the Irular and Kadar Tribes	1996	Mettupalayam Reserve Forest Area and Annamalai Wild Life Sanctuary
8.	A study on the minimum level of scientific knowledge of the common man	1999	2000 people in Madurai City, T.N.
9.	Non-formal education for the school dropout children in the age group of 6 to 14 years	1999	9900 drop-outs in Coimbatore city, T.N.
10.	Adult Education under the NLMP	1988	30,812 illiterates in Perur (1984-92) by 300 Adult Edn. Centres

(Contd...)

1	2	3	4
11.	Training in mass employment generation through MEGSAT	1996	50 persons of Men and Women of low income group
12.	Ten day training programme for Social Animators sponsored by CAPART	1992	100 animators
13.	Migratory trend among the Scheduled Caste people	1994	Coimbatore districts of T.N. (600 sample)
14.	Self concept; Self-esteem and the Level of Aspiration of the SC people	1994	1017 SC people in Coimbatore Districts, T.N.
15.	Housing conditions of the SC People (by ICSSR)	1994	SC people in Coimbatore Districts, T.N.
16.	Problems and future projects of the National Project for Bio-Gal development in TN	1996	Nilgris, Erode, Coimbatore Districts, T.N.
17.	Socio-economic study of Scavangers (by SCD, MSJ & E, Govt. of India)	1998	Mysore, Tumkur and Kolar Districts of Karnataka
18.	Socio-economic study of the Kannikkarars	1998	Kanyakumai Districts, T.N.
19.	Impact of mass communication strategy developed for DWCRA groups	1999	Erode Districts, TN (by AIR, CBE)
20.	Women Entrepreneurship Development project (WEDP)	1999	Women entrepreneurs in Coimbatore Districts
21.	Seven-day Gram Shree Mela (by CAPART and DRDA)	1999	Artisans from all over India
22.	Installation of 55 Borewells in the Drinking Water scarce Village (ARWSP)	1994	Acclerated Water Supply Programme in Coimbatore Districts, T.N.
23.	Urban Basic services for the Poor (UBSP)	1996	UNICEF volunteers in 25 Municipalities and 2 corporation in T.N.
24.	One day workshop on the dimension of social change	1996	Jounalists in Coimbatore Districts, T.N.
25.	National Seminar on Organised Violence against SC in India	1996	90 delegates in UGC seminar

(Contd...)

1	2	3	4
26.	Bio-fertiliser production and popularization among the Tribals	1997	Manar Area, Karamadai Range, T.N.
27.	Production of high yielding Sugarcane through Micropropagation	1997	Anamalai Block of Coimbatore Districts
28.	Construction of Houses for the SCs	1997	Thangamaipuram Village of Theni Districts
29.	Mass production of disease-free high yielding Banana plants through tissue culture	1997	Karamadai Block of Combatore Districts
30.	Piolet scale producing of microbial pesticides for eliminating Orictes Rhinoceros Beetle	1997	Vellingadu Village, Coimbatore Districts

Likewise, some of the projects are Mushroom cultivation, operation of modern agricultural appliances, Awareness of Neem Products, Science and Communication, Training in Computer HW and SW, Tissue culture, AIDS awareness workshop for the NGOs, Screen Printing, Textile mills awareness, Skill development, Cultivation of Medicinal plants, Motor Rewinding, Audio cassette recording, Video shooting, Editing technology awareness, Livestock loss and expenditure, Employment generation of Tribals, Beautycare training and cutting, designing and embroidery products making.etc., are conducted under this CSRTC organization. Apart from the above projects, some of the ongoing NGOs programmes are going on. And this CSR TC conducts Research methodology courses from time to time for research scholars of Universities and other research agencies. And it published a wealth of English and Tamil publications concerned with Educational, Technological and Cultural Issues brought from time to time by the Trust. In 2003, Dec 17-19, a group monitoring workshop was conducted for the National Level STED project implementing organizations at Tiruchirappalli in Tamilnadu. About 40 STED (Science and Technology Entrepreneur's Development) project directors from various states participated in the workshop.

The NGOs' very important functions are:

— Collection of information about the violations

— Education Legislation

— Solidarity

— Working in the areas of Social Rights Utilize the human resources

— Employment activities

In the case of CSRTC which was involved in many subsystem—level employment skill building programmes and the other cooperative forms of activity. Thus social mobilization and concerns about social justice and equity seem to have greater importance for the NGOs than economic efficiency or productivity. This NGO targeted their efforts at the marginalized, socio-economically deprived sections of the community. This NGO follow a long-term approach to self-employment, stressing the importance of sustainable development through people's participation and responsibility sharing in the process of development. It is high time that serious attention is given to the revamping of universities in Tamilnadu. The quality of PG programmes offered in many university departments is so far below the standards of the leading universities in the country. Because of the changing context, the universities are much pressure and now to play different roles—roles that are different from the traditional ones. Instead of the traditional role of preservation, generation and transmission of knowledge, they have to actively participate in the socio-economic development of the country. Significant highlights of these new roles are given below:

- Providing educational programmes of new models based on flexibility and learner choice;
- Preparing students for information era by developing the skill for information processing;
- Preparing students for life-long learning by developing an appropriate learning style among them;

- Providing for adult and non-formal education in an increasing percentage of mature learners with the help of NGOs;
- Providing for specialised skill-oriented courses of different levels by the different NGOs.
- Catering to the demands of the international market by some self-supporting workshops through NGOs.
- Maintaining quality in all the above endeavours.
- Optimising the available resources to facilitate quality output.

The above highlights indicate that the universities have a crucial role to play in providing not only access to higher education but quality education to more people with less resources adding an international dimension. It is therefore very important that the universities respond rather urgently to these changing contexts with NGOs and the changes expectations. Unless the universities are a little more positive and proactive with the changing society, the damage will be too much and may need to long too recover.

REFERENCES

1. http:// www. Aiuweb.org
2. Noorjahan Bava., (1997) *Non-Governmental Organisations in Development*, Kanishka Pub., New Delhi. pp. 209-211.
3. Nachimuthu, K et al (1990) Enrolment and Employment in Higher Education, *International Educator*, Thiruvananthapuram, Kerala.
4. Sareen, N (2005), *Information and Communication Technology*, Anmol Pub. Pvt Ltd, New Delhi, p. 332.

26

Bridging the Gap between Theory and Practice through Participation

S. Sumathi

Generally there is a gap between academic and practical. This is the difference between precept and practice. Success lies in bridging this gap. As social scientists we teach several theoretical frameworks and models of development. Most of these are used as explanations for the practical social phenomena. Mostly these are *post-facto* explanations. Thus still the gap between the theory and practice remains without overcoming the gap. People tend to forget that the theory was nothing but the outcome of practice. With the result, theoretical knowledge has been kept out of the reach of voiceless and completely controlled by the researchers. In many developing countries information centres are almost entirely out of the reach of relatively powerless groups. Even in North America, the centre of information industry, there is a vast storehouse of knowledge about people's lives that is often beyond the ready access of those affected by it (Gaventa John, Merrifield Juliet, 1984). The situation is no way different in stratified India. As much as others subjugated some human groups, others subjugate some knowledge systems in the course of human history. Hierarchisation of knowledge systems is reflected and manifested in several ways.

The knowledge system has been kept in a hierarchy and completely controlled by the dominant sectors.

"The researcher develops knowledge based on data collected from individuals, groups and organisations in a social setting. Those individuals, groups and organisations do not have any control over the knowledge generated and obtained from them. They are only the 'objects' of research". (Tandon Rajesh, 2002).

Action Research, Applied Research and Operational Research have been linked with 'problem solving', its goal will be linked with the future of 'problem solving' itself. That the notion of 'problem' in organisational studies is itself problematic has been pointed out by the researchers (Landry, 1995). But this concept of 'problem solving' has been criticised by the participatory researchers later on. In recent times the use of participatory method both as a theoretical framework and as an applicable module is gaining importance. However Participatory Method is the most abused one. Its meaning differed considerably, both in theory and practice, from context to context. It should be noted here that Participatory Research is an integrated process, which stands on a common platform of theory and practice. Often times Participatory Research is used as an instant method like the fast foods. In addition, Participatory Research is increasingly becoming arbitrary to suit the needs and goals of the organizations or agencies. The utilization of PRA/PLA method is so arbitrary that it only rationalizes what was being done earlier and what is being done today. This kind of lessaize-faire method creates further gap between the theory and practice within the Participatory Mode.

In this chapter an attempt is made to bring out the varying meanings and use of Participatory Mode by the stakeholders who are involved in the process of development. At one level I am trying to bring about theoretical understanding about the concept of participation. I am also presenting my experiences in the field of Participatory Research and the attitude of multilateral agencies, NGOs that may provide an understanding from practical point of view.

Participation as a Theory

'Participation' today is a byword for the development rhetoric. Development literature is replete with 'participation' as a process or a product. 'Participation' has acquired a wide range of meanings over time. One end of the spectrum of meanings is the use of participation as a means of data collection and on the other end is the use of participation as a process providing the powerless the power to choose from. William Foote Whyte was one of the early sociologists associated with Participatory Action Research (PAR) and comment about the subject's neglect of social action in favour of social structure (Whyte, 1959). He raised several methodological questions as well as questions concerning the goals of the social science (Whyte, 1991). PAR has emerged as a critique of other forms of social research, namely, 'the standard model of social research' where 'research' and 'action' are sought to be kept separate, and the model of action research controlled by the researcher'...(Whyte, 19991, p. 273). Hence, Participatory Action Researchers looked at PAR modules as a alternative research method drawn by him/herself.

A cursory look at the literature certainly suggests that the term 'Participatory' means several things to several people. This depends on the ideological plank on which one stands. The variations and wide variety of meanings attributed to the term "participatory" have been systematised to some extent by Jules Perry (1995) and classified into seven different participation: Manipulative participation, Passive participation, Participation by consultation, Participation for material incentives, Functional participation, Interactive participation and Self-mobilisation.

Theoretically, this classification is comprehensive enough to encompass all the meanings attributed to "participatory". The main conceptual framework of participation has been drawn by Holland and Blackburn (1998), White (1999), Tandon (2002), Govinda and Diwan (2003), and Tandon and Mohanty (2003). Besides, several other works (for instance Freire, 1972, 1976; Chambers, 1983, 1995) which had great influence on the debate, at least two-decade-old on the meaning and practice of people's participation.

There are certain main issues have been taken for granted in to the process of participation at the theoretical level. The most crucial are developmental strategies. Brown (1985), when focusing an analytical viewpoint about the alternative theories and strategies says;

> "Participatory research offers a strategy for local education, research, and organisation that is consistent with the assumptions of people-centred development. It encourages inquiry that focuses on local problems and pragmatic concerns. It provides education that encourages activist attitude and informal collective action. It builds organisations that enable cohesive local action and link groups to the larger context beyond the village". (p. 98)

Another major issue attached to Participatory is, the local community participation. There are several different meanings attributed to community participation. According to Govinda and Diwan (2003) there are two main meanings imputed to community participation. One is the understanding that the community is reluctant to participate, and hence it should be brought to the centre stage to participate. This kind of community participation, thus, has a functional meaning. The second meaning attributed is that community participation loosens the rigid administrative framework, as there is a pressure from the bottom. Further they also point out the difficulty of defining a "community" when they say;

> "Community" is obviously not a homogenous notion. It is either various communities unequally and differently placed within a society, or various groups in a community unequally placed.... Community could be viewed in two different perspective: (1) local class-caste composition ...(2) elected representatives where their class composition influences the nature of involvement as well as the nature of conflict arising from such involvement ... By implication, community participation has also to be viewed in a localised manner. (p. 14)

It is acutely important to note that often what is considered a community is composed of hierarchically placed unequal groups. In such situations the use of the blanket term of 'community participation' fails to capture the reality. Taking such realities into account, it becomes clear that the participation by local community is partial reflecting the inequalities. Similarly Meredith (1999), while sharing her observation about the partnership between farmers and scientists in Napal says;

> "The gulf between grassroots training participants and facilitators is often wide, when the groups come from vastly different cultural and socio-economic backgrounds. Facilitators can do much to narrow the gap by redefining implied relationships and roles. In traditional patriarchal or colonial learning situations, the facilitator/teacher arrives to 'bestow knowledge on the uniformed'. Such a one-way transfer of information encourages a hierarchical relationship between teacher and students. Equalising the relationship from the beginning should be the first goal in participatory training settings." (p. 233)

Theoretically the concepts "participation" and "empowerment" are intricately interlinked and reflect understandings about the nature of power. In Freire's (1972) concept of power implies that by necessity the oppressed must appropriate for themselves, power which has hitherto been in the possession of the powerful. He suggests 'Dialogue' as inquiry and intervention described by him as a liberating mechanism in the process of knowing and changing. This process ultimately provides a sense of empowerment among the powerless. Tandon (1979) while explaining the case, the rural situation and the process of empowerment among the peer group leaders which intern created more initiatives and become more empowered, ultimately the village situation underwent changes. Hence, by definition people alone can empower themselves and participation is the means for such process.

Participation as a Method

Participatory mode as a methodological tool is used by various organizations with different agendas. Participatory methodology, no matter in what varying sense it is used, has a very definite meaning in the context of development, as perceived by the funding agencies. White (1999) as he was talking about the participation says:

"Authentic participation of grassroots people may still be more an ideal than a reality. Individuals and agencies actively engaged in development are conscientiously struggling to move beyond just talking in order to achieve this ideal" (p.17).

Whatever be the ideology of grassroots people, the ultimate process of development lies with the political will. It is also important here to understand the fact that the very concept of development is closely related to the political ideology. However, there are several organizations, which utilize the "Participatory Methods" the context of development in de-politesse meaning. Development and participatory development in a political sense cannot be treated separately. Participatory method opposed the patriarchal and top-down approach to development. Facilitation and advocacy are the concepts that have been extensively used in the process of people centered development. Nielsen and Kiiti (1999) while defining the role of facilitator and the advocate at the practical level;

"We often hear phrases such as, "we are going to facilitate a workshop on farmer exchange, or 'they are advocating the use of contraceptives for family planning.'.... A fine distinction was drawn between advocacy and facilitation by many. The most explicit distinction was that an advocate is often driven by an 'external agenda' while the facilitator seeks to understand and help people determine their own agenda." (p.52)

In a sense this method was trying to eliminate the setting in of the dependency syndrome. In fact, the participatory mode if practiced in its truest meaning will also pave the way for the sustainability of the process of planning, identification of the problems, prioritization and finding solutions within the context of the available resources. Sustainability is the crucial factor in development. If the process is not sustainable, it is not development at all. Often participation as a methodology is used more to manufacture the consent of the people. It definitely serves in that sense the "needs" of the agencies, be it governmental or otherwise, implementing the important elements in participatory research:

1. It is required on the part of the facilitator (or facilitating team) the awareness of one's own limitations, a sense of insecurity and one's relative ignorance (compared with the local people involved). In addition to this one needs consciousness of oneself as working with certain values, this may differ considerably from those of the local people.
2. Accepting one's relative ignorance, trying to learn from the people concerned through empathy and friendship about their problems and needs.
3. Understanding the overall political economy in the village or area concerned as perceived by the local community(ies).
4. After acquiring sufficient knowledge about the problems further dialogue with the local people and facilitating a search together for possible solutions. Since most problems are due to conflicts of interest existing in the village or area concerned, it is important not to ignore—but rather to discover—such conflicts and underlying social structural contradictions. It is needed to bring them into the open and initiate discussions to overcome the existing contradictions.

Participatory research mostly is aimed to find solutions to concrete problems and conflicts. The outcome of such participatory research, if carried out consistently, will contribute to a knowledge base of conflict-solving methods applicable to varying situations. The participatory research methods have contributed to awakening the poor and vulnerable people's awareness about the conflicts and contradictions existing in their situation and ways to overcome these. Researchers often play the role of facilitators and share their knowledge with the people they work with, helping the people to interpret more accurately their own situation. Such research could direct itself simultaneously towards the development of theories and to the solution of concrete social problems. Tandon (1981), rightly says;

> "The values of the researchers have to be in congruence with the values of the participatory approach. He has to believe in the basic strengths of the people and has to cherish democratic values in the proper sense of term. The behaviour skills required to encourage and sustain participation of people must be possessed by the researchers. These behaviour skills become critical in the context of the focus on the underprivileged sections of our population. Since a dominant characteristic of the underprivileged is their inability to and fear of participation, greater effort is required to facilitate the participation of such section". (p. 38)

Participation as I See It

I am presenting my experiences in the field of 'Participatory Research' and making this presentation entirely in first person and in a simple narrative style. This will facilitate, I hope, in describing my experiences in this field with specific reference to my work among the *Malayali* Tribe of Tamil Nadu. The use of the term Participatory is very much wide in its meaning and scope. To put it simply at one end of the spectrum of meanings attributed to 'participation' is the generation of 'manufactured consent' and at the other end of the spectrum is the meaning that it is a total bottom-up approach. Between these two polarised understandings, there are several variations in between. Often it is seen that the meaning participation is restricted as a *product* rather than *process*. It is also seen often that participation is restricted to using PRA techniques to collect, as part of an extractive process, data at the bottom. This is used basically in planning from the top. This kind of an approach is often used by multilateral agencies, NGOs and so on. This is also becoming a standard mode of developmental strategies of governmental agencies in recent times.

My experience of associating with Participatory Research is short (about ten years) and three projects long. I would like to very briefly express my experience of Participatory Research before presenting the case study with which I was deeply involved. The first project was a UNICEF-sponsored multi-disciplinary project on reduction of anaemia among urban poor of Tamil Nadu. The core group of the project—which included urban planners, economists, epidemiologists and anthropologists—agreed to use a participatory mode in generating plans for and execution of the interventions by the people themselves. This project had an initial phase of Base-line Survey (BLS) of about six month and an eighteen-month phase of intervention followed by a three month evaluation.

The base-line survey was conducted independently for the epidemiological and anthropological parameters separately. The basic outcome of the BLS was supposed to be ploughed back to the people so that they could take part in planning sufficiently informed about the problem. The intervention phase was the weakest link in terms of participation. The involvement of the community in this phase was minimal. Even after mid-course corrections—when the clustering approach was followed — the local community could not *own* this problem and could be perceived or recorded. The major lesson that stood at the end of the project, was that a project with participatory mode should provide enabling conditions for the local communities to participate as equal partners and know their priorities and evolve solutions. This project precisely failed on this count.

The second participatory project I was (and still I am) associated with was "The Grass-roots level Democracy and Dalits". This is basically a study of the constitutionally guaranteed Panchayat system (as a consequence of 73rd Amendment of Constitution of India) and the participatory democracy at the grassroots. The Constitution guarantees political positions to historically marginalised and oppressed groups such as the Scheduled Castes, Scheduled Tribes and women. The traditional rural landed-class controlled both economic and political institutions. As a result some communities remained excluded from the local political institutions. The ritual inequalities, thus, were also reflected in the inequality of political power. To overcome this skewed situation, the Constitution Amendment was brought about. Basically this is meant to provide conditions for political participation.

The study with which I was associated tried to understand the ground realities of political participation by *dalit* groups. I, along with a colleague of mine, has been following the political process in one village panchayat the president's post of which was reserved for SC. So far we have been following the political dynamics of that village panchayat for six years. Since 1996 to the present, the election for the post of president in this village panchayat (Pappapatti in Madurai district of Tamil Nadu) was announced nineteen times and only three times nominations could be filed. Two times the candidate elected assumed office and within hours resigned. The third time the election was countermand as one of the candidates died.

In the case of the two participatory projects with which I am associated (as presented), I was a third party. I, nor my associates, had any role in choosing the methodology. In both the cases the avowed objective was to use a participatory method to achieve a goal. The meanings and actual ground-level techniques used were different. With this experience of mine, a team joined together and started working towards a participatory planning and programming mode. This was done after a one-year long discussion with the sponsors who assured us that they would not interfere with the process.

We made a quick reconnoitre of a small area in the Javadhu Hills Block of Thiruvannamalai district of TN, and one village—Elanthampattu—was selected. The selection was based on the relative isolation, small and culturally homogeneous village. This was a Malayali tribal village with 68 households. The anthropologist-facilitators started spending good lot of time daily with the community for almost three months. The community was told that the purpose of their visits was to observe and generate whatever information the people think right. It took three months for the people to believe the words of the facilitators when they offered to construct a hut for the facilitators.

The basic norms followed by the facilitators included:

(a) Being sensitive to the problems of the community.

(b) Considering the interacting graphs including the community, other facilitators and governmental agencies should be treated as equals.

(c) Essentially the data is generative rather than extractive and not by the researchers (facilitators).

(d) Participation is basically a means rather than an end in itself and thus it is a social process.

Some of the major PRA techniques were used to generate data basically bring together the life ways of the community. In fact we facilitated in putting together the ethnography by the community itself. We also facilitated the local community to identify their major problems and possible solutions. The community has also prioritised their problems in terms of those, which have to be tackled first, and those latter. It took about six months for the facilitators to document and put together the information provided by the community. This document (Tamil), was called "People's ethnography". This was again ploughed back to the community for their approval and owning the data. It took sometime before they started discussing among themselves. They have suggested some corrections, explanations and omissions of certain information and so on. The facilitators carried out these suggestions and document was placed before the Panchayat of the village. This initial process has provided confidence in both the community and the facilitators on each other. It also paved the way for greater interaction and respect for the viewpoint of each other.

This was the time when we discussed with the people for a stakeholders' meeting. When the community agreed, we approached the government officials of the line departments at the district level. After getting the consent a one-day stakeholders' workshop was held in the field itself. All the representatives of 68 households of the village, the tribal panchayat leaders, the government officials, the NGO and the anthropologist-facilitators attended this meeting. The meeting itself was conducted deliberately as between equals. There was no stage; no garlanding and all the stakeholders were sitting in a circle. The meeting started with the presentation of "The

People's Report". This was followed by the presentation of the community about specific issues. The local MLA also expressed her views. This was followed by the presentation and clarifications by the government officials. There were some definitive programmes drawn up by the officials.

Within the next one-month, based on the people's report and the deliberations at the stakeholders' workshop, there were quite a few questions at the community-facilitators level and the local-level representatives of the line departments about how to operationalise the conclusions reached? It was quite clear that dovetailing the needs with already existing programmes of the government could solve some issues raised at the workshop. There are some needs and priorities of the community, which could be worked with the help of NGO, which is working there. There were yet some more issues, which need to be tackled only by the community itself. As a part of the existing governmental plans, some of the immediate priorities of Malayali tribes of Elanthampattu like the basic health issues could be tackled. In fact, the Deputy Director health has suggested training the local women as *Dai* (mid-wife).

The NGO, which is working in the area, has taken up issues concerning education when the local educated youth were appointed as education facilitators. While the first priority of the local community was laying a path from the down hill to the village. This was the first priority of the community. But this required a clear joint effort of both the local community and the forest department. Since the village is within the reserve forest there is a need to have the approval of the department to lay the path. Since the area closer to the village is patta land of the local community, they have to transfer that land for laying the path. The local NGO and the anthropologist-facilitators facilitated this process. The actual process of laying path took about three months.

With this experience, we have extended this process to ten more villages in the same Panchayat. It was the opinion of the community that they should be provided the skills to improve their income. SHGs were formed and they are today involved in schemes for alternate income generation. The SHGs themselves entrusted the job of maintaining the accounts, writing letters and dealing with other agencies to one of the educated members and she is doing the job well. Similarly through a campaign mode enrolment of children was done during that year. The education facilitators who are within the community itself motivated and brought together the children, teachers and parents in this effort. In addition adult education centres were started and the local educated youth were trained to conduct classes for basic skills in reading and numeracy. The local community overwhelmingly welcomed this, as the facilitators were their own children.

At different stages resource persons were invited to talk, interact, provide inputs to the local community. For instance, a practising resource persons of SHGs was invited to share her experience, discuss the intricacies and motivate the local community. Similarly the resource persons were invited to interact and suggest modification, if any, during the course of practising various programmes. Similarly the resource persons of Makkal Palli Iyakkam (The People's School Organisation) were interacting with children, parents and education facilitators to operationalise "Joy of Learning". Looking back at our experience, I can say confidently that we are successful in initiating the social process of participatory planning and achieving. In terms of the basic features (as we understand) of the process of participation, the following are the important ones:

1. Participatory mode is a means and not an end in itself.
2. Participatory mode means a bottom-up approach both for obtaining community's consent as well as planning.
3. A definitive role for the community in translating the plans to executable actions.
4. Any programme with participatory mode should provide enabling conditions for the local communities to participate as equal partners.

Of the above, what were followed closely and what could not be followed determine how successful or otherwise the participatory process was.

The *positive aspects* of the participatory process initiated are:

— The community shared its socio-cultural, economic and other knowledge and the facilitators interacted with the community as equals.

— There was no hidden agenda of the community-facilitators and the community was convinced that the facilitators are only assisting the community to record their way of life, their problems and priorities.

— The community does the process of planning and working out the solutions, with facilitative assistance. It has thus, initiated a bottom-up process.

The *aspects*, which limited the participatory process, are:

— Largely the basic framework for development is predetermined and the influence of the governmental agencies is considerable.

— Similarly, the influence of the NGO sponsoring the project (?) is also considerable. The NGO basically believes in the top-down approach and thus negating the participatory approach. The NGO accepts the participatory approach as a method to collect data but to be utilised for a top-down planning.

REFERENCES

1. Brown, L. David., 1985. "People-Centred Development and Participatory Research", *Hasrvard Educational Review,* Vol. 55, No. 1, pp. 69-75.
2. Chambers, R., 1983. *Rural Development: Putting the Last First,* London: Longman.
3. 1995. "Poverty and Livelihood: Whose Reality Counts?", *IDS Discussion Paper No. 347,* University of Sussex: IDS, January.
4. 1997. *Whose Reality Counts? Putting the First Last,* London.
5. Freire, P. 1972. *Pedagogy of the Oppressed,* New York: Seabury Press.

6. 976. *Education for Critical Consciousness*, New York: Seabury Press.

7. Gaventa John and Merrifield Juliet, 1984. "Participatory Research in North America and India" in Tandon, Rajesh (ed) *Participatory Research: Revisiting the Roots*, New Delhi: Mosaic Books, 122-37.

8. Govinda, R and Reshmi Diwan (eds). 2003. *Community Participation and Empowerment in Primary Education*, New Delhi: Sage Publication.

9. Holland, Jeremy and James Blackburn (eds). 1998. *Whose Voice: Participatory Research and Policy Change*, London: Intermediate Technology Publications.

10. Landry. M. (1995). A Note on the Concept of 'Problem'. *Organisation Studies*, 6,2, pp. 315-43.

11. Narayan, Pradeep. 2003. "Empowerment through participation", *EPW*, vol. xxxviii, no. 25, pp. 2484-86.

12. Sumathi, S and V. Sudarsen. 2005. "What Does the New Panchayat System Guarantee? A Case Study of Pappapatti", *EPW*, Vol. XL, No. 34, pp. 3751-58.

13. Sudarsen,V, S.Sumathi and P.I.Prabhakar. 2005. "Methodological Issues of Participatory Health Care Management: A Case Study of Maternal Anaemia Among the Urban Poor of Tamil Nadu", in Dalal, K. Ajit and Subha Ray (eds) *Social Dimensions of Health*, Delhi: Rawat, pp. 346-61.

14. Tandon, Rajesh. 2002. "Dialogue", in Tandon, Rajesh (ed) *Participatory Research: Revisiting the Roots*, New Delhi: Mosaic Books, 275-94.

15. Tandon, Rajesh (ed). 2002. *Participatory Research: Revisiting the Roots*, New Delhi: Mosaic Books.

16. Tandon, Rajesh and Ranjita Mohanty (eds). *Does Civil Society Matter: Governance in Contemporary India*, New Delhi: Sage Publication.

17. Whyte, W.F. (1959), *Man and Organisation*, Irwin, Homewood.

18. (1989). "Introduction to the Special issue on Action Research for the Twenty-first Century: Participation, Reflection, and Practice". *American Behaviour Scientiest*, 32,5. pp. 502-12.

19. (1991). "*Social Theory for Action: How Individuals and Organisations Learn to Change*, Sage, Newbury Park, CA.

27

Dissemination of Development Measures

Role of Universities and NGOs

P. Adinarayana Reddy
Uma Devi

India is the second largest country in the world in terms of population and seventh in-terms of areas. It is also richest in terms of culture and natural resources. Further one-third of the scientific manpower of world are Indians. On the other hand half of our rural peoples are living below poverty line, about 40 per cent of them are illiterates, more than half of the children enrolled in Ist class are dropped before they reach 5th class, more than one-fourth of the workers are under-employed, high unemployment rate etc., i.e. prevalent in the country. As a result of these diversities, one can see the inequality in all spears of the society and individuals in particular. The gap between haves and have-nots are increasing with the increase of population. No doubt, the Government has taken adequate measures to reduce the gap and to provide equal opportunities for the all for sustainable development by launching of Welfare Programmes. The programmes are directed to general population and as well as for specific groups.

The scope of the programmes are very wide and scattered in terms of implementations. For the convenience, the important programmes implemented by the government are grouped under three major groups viz., the programmes meant for SC/ST and OBCs, women and farmers. The programmes are as follows.

I. The Welfare Programmes for the SC, ST & OBCs

1. Grant-in-Aid to Voluntary Organisations Working for Scheduled Castes.
2. Assistance to NGO's Working for SC, ST and OBC.
3. Liberation and Rehabilitation of Scavengers.
4. Pre-Matric Scholarship to the Children of those engaged in Unclean Occupations.
5. Pre-Matric Scholarship for OBCs.
6. Post-Matric Scholarship for SC/ST students.
7. Integrated Programme for Street Children.
8. Hostel for Scheduled Caste Boys and Girls.
9. Book Banks for SC/ST students.
10. Pre-Examination Coaching for other backward classes.
11. Multi-Sectoral Development Plans for Minorities.
12. Maulana Azad Education Foundation's Schemes for Educationally Backward Minorities.
13. Financial Assistance through National Scheduled Castes and Scheduled Tribes Finance and Development Corporation.
14. Financial Assistance through National Safai Karmacharis Finance and Development Corporation.
15. Financial Assistance through National Minorities Development and Finance Corporation.
16. Indira Awas Yojna (IAY).
17. Jawahar Gram Samriddhi Yojana (JGSY)
18. Scheme for SC/ST/Other Farmers.
19. Schemes in Handloom Sectors.
20. Special Component Plan (SCP) and Tribal Sub-Plan (TSP).
21. Welfare of SCs/STs/Weaker Sections through Bio-Technological Process/Technique.

22. National Overseas Scholarship for SC & ST candidates.

II. **Welfare Programmes for the Farmers**

1. Integrated Cereals Development Programme in Rice based Cropping Systems Areas (ICDP-RICE).
2. Foundation & Certified Seed Production of Vegetable Crops.
3. Transport Subsidy for the Movement of Seeds to the North Eastern States, Sikkim, H. P., J & K, Hill Areas of U. P. and W. B.
4. Oil Palm Development Programme (OPDP).
5. Accelerated Maize Development Programme (AMDP).
6. Oilseeds Production Programme (OPP).
7. National Pulses Development Project (NPDP).
8. Promotion of Integrated Pest Management.
9. Sustainable Development of Sugarcane Based Cropping System (SUBACS).
10. Special Jute Development Programme (SJDP).
11. Intensive Cotton Development Programme (ICDP) under Mini-Mission-II of Technology.
12. Mission on Cotton.
13. National Project on Development and use of Bio-Fertilisers Commercial Floriculture.
14. Development of Vegetables.
15. Integrated Development of Cashewnut.
16. Integrated Development of Coconut industry In India.
17. Development of Cocoa.
18. Development of Medicinal and Aromatic Plants.
19. Mushroom Cultivation.

20. Integrated Programme for Development of Spices
21. Use of Plastics in Agriculture
22. Integrated Development of Tropical, Temperate and Arid Zone Fruits

III. Welfare Programmes for the Women

1. Rashtriya Mahila Kosh.
2. Swayamsiddha Yojana (IWEP)
3. Employment-cum-Income Generating Unit for Women (NORAD).
4. Support to Training and Employment Programme for Women (STEP).
5. Empowering Women through Education.
6. Women's Education.
7. Short Duration Education Courses for Women.
8. Short Stay Homes for Women and Girls.
9. National Creche Fund Scheme, 1994.
10. General Grant-in-aid Scheme for Assistance to NGOs/ Voluntary Organisations.
11. Creche and Hostel for Working Women.
12. Organisational Assistance to Voluntary Organisation for Women and Child Development.
13. Grant-in-aid for Research, Publications and Monitoring.
14. Assistance to Voluntary Organisation for Prevention of Atrocities on Women.
15. Vocational Training Programme for Women.
16. Assstance for Economic Empowerment.
17. Working Women's Hostels.
18. Creches.
19. Family Counselling Centers.
20. National Social Assistance Programme.

21. Reproductive and Child Health.
22. Science and Technology for Women.
23. Mahila Coir Yojana.
24. Projects under Bio-technology Based Programmes for Women and Rural Development.
25. Mahila Vikas Nidhi (Enterprise Promotion).
26. Micro Credit Scheme (Entrepreneur Development).
27. Balika Samriddhi Yojana.
28. Death Relief and Rehabilitation Fund Scheme.
29. Rajrajeshwari Mahila Kalyan Bima Yojana.

Recognising the inequalities among different sections of the society in different area, the Government of India have formulated the above programmes for the benefit of the various sections of the population and are being sponsored and implemented by different agencies. The success of development oriented programmes lies in the participation of the target and reaching the benefits to the target. This is possible only if the targets are aware about the programmes and also the programme implementing authority should be conscious of similar programmes so as to avoid the duplication of the programmes leading to the wastage of men, materials and resources.

No doubt the government is propagating about the welfare measures initiated for the benefit of the target. However, these efforts are found to be inadequate and benefit are being utilized by the pseudo beneficiaries. Hence creation of awareness among the people about the government's policies, programmes is very important task in successful implementation of the development programmes.

Apart from the Government machinery, the task of implementation of the welfare programmes are assigned to the Non-Government agencies popularly known as voluntary organisation. These are the organisations created by a group of people with a definite objectives. They are autonomous, less rigid in terms of administration known to the community, aware of the problems of the community and capable of eliciting the participation of the community in their activities. Recognising the potentialities of these agencies almost all the ministries/ department has created scope for these agencies and made partners of the programmes. In other words after government, the NGOs have large network and capable of penetrating into any and all spears of the community. Hence these are the right agencies that can take up the task of creation of awareness among the people about the various efforts made by the Government for their welfare.

In addition to the above, the higher education system especially the Universities, with vast human resources, with different specialisation are also participating in the development of the community at various levels. After recognising the extension as the third dimension of the Universities, all the faculties are reorienting themselves for outreach activities. Traditionally Universities are involved in teaching and conducting research only. However the findings of the research is limited to the papers and now through the outreach activities started to dessiminate among the community.

From the above it is clear that apart from Government the Universities and NGOs are the major agencies involved in welfare of the society. Hence if both the agencies works together there will be effective dissemination of information and possibility of enhanced participation of the target in the development programmes. The Universities and NGOs can work at 3 levels. At the first level they can create awareness about the programs by using different strategies based on the available manpower and technology either by adopting a particular area or a section of population. In the second stage they can act as catalyst and encourage the target to participate and utilize the programmes for their advantage. In the third stage they themselves can implement the programmes independently or through network.

The Universities and NGOs can share the information and competencies available with them in dissemination of information on welfare programmes. However in case of implementation, they should keep in view about its competencies before volunteering into the implementation of the welfare programmes. To be specific the functions of the Universities and NGOs in dissemination of the welfare programmes are as follows :

Universities

1. Identifying needs of the community and collect information relating to the various developmental programmes.
2. Organise awareness campaigns in the selected areas on selected themes by the related departments.
3. The students and faculty should act as resource persons in creation of awareness about the programmes.
4. The universities can conduct action research to identify the deficiencies in the implementation of the ongoing programmes and findings should be supplied to the implementation authorities for improving the quality of the programmes.
5. Universities can help the programme administration in selecting the targets, and providing feedback about the performance of the programme.
6. The efficiency of the programme functionaries can be improved by conducting pre-service and in-service training programmes.

Role of NGOs

The NGOs being peoples organisation can play a significant role in dissimination of the developmental programmes and in enhancing the participation of the target in the programmes by adopting the following strategies.

— Mouth to mouth communication.

— By using traditional and modern media.

— Organising village meets.

— Organising sandy meets.

— Involving the beneficiaries of a particular programme in dessemінating information about other programmes.
— Through SHG leaders.
— Inviting the functionaries of the developmental departments to interact with their beneficiaries.
— Developing documentation on developmental programmes or collecting information from different sources and spreading the same among the community.

Index

□□□